FAMILY WALKS
IN HEREFORD
AND WORCESTER

Gordon Ottewell

Scarthin Books, Cromford, Derbyshire   1988

FAMILY WALKS
IN HEREFORD AND WORCESTER

Family Walks Series
General Editor: Norman Taylor

———————

THE COUNTRY CODE
Guard against all risk of fire
Fasten all gates
Keep dogs under proper control
Keep to paths across farm land
Avoid damaging fences, hedges and walls
Leave no litter
Safeguard water supplies
Protect wildlife, wild plants and trees
Go carefully along country roads
Respect the life of the countryside

———————

Published by Scarthin Books, Cromford, Derbyshire

Phototypesetting, printing by Higham Press Ltd., Shirland, Derbyshire

ISBN 0 907758 20 7

Dedication

This book is dedicated to the memory of a dear friend, Gordon Simmons, teacher, naturalist and countryman, who helped me to discover this treasured landscape.

UNDERHILL FARM (Route 10)

1

PREFACE

I discovered the countryside of Hereford & Worcester during my college days and have returned to delight in it countless times since. It has been no easy task to select a representative collection of walks - many areas have of necessity been omitted, others have scarcely been touched - one of the dilemmas of having to choose!

The countryside is constantly changing, not always for the better. I was reminded of the rapidity of this process recently when returning to a village through which I had routed one of the walks for my book on Family Walks in the Cotswolds two years ago. I had illustrated the walk with a photograph of an old ivy-covered railway bridge and discovered to my chagrin that it had disappeared!

Whatever the changes however, Hereford & Worcester will remain a walker's paradise. The paths can be elusive at times but the rewards from persevering to find and follow them are rich indeed. Families who leave their cars behind and use their legs tend in my experience to be happy families, so happy walking in Hereford & Worcester!

Acknowledgements

I should like to thank the following for their help with this book:

Miss E. Lois Barefield, Hon. Sec. Mapping Section, Malvern Hills District Footpath Society.

Mr. John Poole, Administrator, the Worcestershire Nature Conservation Trust.

Mr. David Gorvett.

Margaret, my wife, for typing the manuscript and giving constant encouragement.

G.O.

About the author

Gordon Ottewell lives on the 'wrong' side of the Gloucestershire border with Hereford & Worcester. He writes on country matters in the 'Gloucestershire Echo'. His country books include:

'A Hereford & Worcester Quiz Book' (Barn Owl Books).
'Family Walks in the Cotswolds' (Scarthin Books).
'Wildlife Walks in the North Cotswolds' (Thornhill Press).
'A Cotswold Quiz Book' (Barn Owl Books).
'Gloucestershire - A County Quiz Book' (Barn Owl Books).
'Warde Fowler's Countryside' (Severn House).

CONTENTS

MAP OF THE AREA

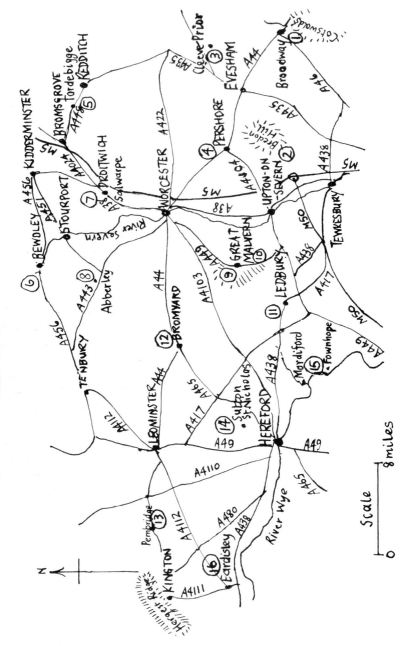

INTRODUCTION

This book is intended to encourage and help families with young children to explore the countryside of Hereford & Worcester on foot. The walks, which range in length from 2½ to 7½ miles, are routed through some of the most delightful parts of the county, and vary considerably in difficulty. As the main aim is to enable children not merely to endure, but to enjoy each walk, their needs and interests are given priority throughout. This means that, wherever possible, a pub or similar source of refreshment is situated roughly midway along the route, which in most cases ends with an easy stretch of downhill or level walking.

Under the heading 'Attractions', mention is made of a few of the features along each route which are likely to appeal to children. That bane of childhood, tiredness through boredom, is far less likely to occur when children are interested and actively involved, so this section includes notes on the history and wild life of the locality, as well as such possible sources of interest as folk stories, unusual objects seen along the way, and so on.

Choosing a walk

Unless the children taking part are experienced walkers, it is advisable to choose fairly easy walks first. The appendix at the end of the book grades the walks in order of difficulty and reference to this will help to avoid the mistake of making excessive demands on children's keenness and stamina. In any case, children will relish the anticipation of tackling more strenuous walks later. With very young children, it may be best to walk part of the route to begin with, or to arrange for the party to be picked up at some point on the route.

Allowing sufficient time

Each walk is intended as the best part of a day's outing, allowing time for play, exploring, and rest stops. It is better to over-estimate rather than under-estimate the time required - there is nothing worse than having to route-march the last stages of the journey. As a rough guide, allow a pace of around a mile per hour for very young children, graduating to two miles per hour for the experienced ten-year-old.

What to wear

The notorious British climate being what it is, it is advisable to go walking prepared for the worst! Sturdy, comfortable shoes or walking boots are preferable to wellingtons, which tire and chafe on long walks. Waterproof outer-garments, such as cagoules, are essential, while underneath, several layers of thin jumpers are better than one thick garment, as they allow more flexibility when weather conditions change. Headgear - caps and bobble hats - should not be overlooked. And don't forget a roomy rucksack in which to carry food and drink, spare clothing, maps, guides, and so on.

Finding the way

Most of the walking will be along public footpaths, with short stretches of road-walking where unavoidable. The route-maps are drawn to a scale of 2½ inches to a mile and if used in conjunction with the route directions should be straightforward to follow. Many walkers will wish to take Ordnance Survey maps along also, and the numbers of the relevant sheets are included in the text. Occasionally, especially after a summer's growth, some stiles along public footpaths become overgrown. A walking stick can be extremely useful at these times to clear a path. Sometimes too, ploughing, or some other farming activity may cause the path to be obscured. Should this occur, take the shortest possible detour round the edge of the field to regain the path.

Refreshments

Most of the pubs en route allow children accompanied by adults into their premises. Some also have beer gardens or play areas, while others are situated near a village green or similar open space. If packed lunches are carried, remember that most landlords do not approve of such food being consumed on the premises. Closing-times should be borne in mind, especially on Sundays. Aim to arrive before 2.00 p.m. on weekdays and 1.00 p.m. on Sundays, if you are buying lunch, as catering often ceases well before closing-time. Teashops usually remain open until five or six o'clock during the summer months.

Public transport

Although it is assumed that most people will travel to the area by car, the starts of some of the walks can be reached by bus. Where available, brief details of local bus services are given with the walk descriptions and addresses of bus operators are included in the appendix.

BROADWAY TOWER (Route 1)

Symbols used on the route maps

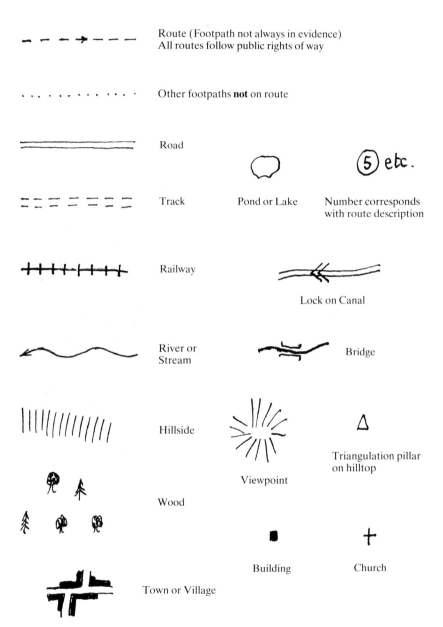

Route (Footpath not always in evidence)
All routes follow public rights of way

Other footpaths **not** on route

Road

Track

Pond or Lake

(5) etc.

Number corresponds
with route description

Railway

Lock on Canal

River or
Stream

Bridge

Hillside

Viewpoint

Triangulation pillar
on hilltop

Wood

Building

Church

Town or Village

A Cotswold Corner

Outline   Broadway Village ~ Bury End ~ Coneygree Lane ~ Broadway Tower Country Park ~ Broadway village.

Summary   This route is intended to provide a taste of hill walking in the small but scenic corner of the Cotswolds that lies within the borders of Hereford & Worcester. Broadway, the starting point, is generally accepted as being one of England's most beautiful villages and although its popularity has exacted a heavy price in terms of the trappings of tourism, there is still much to enjoy.

     The walk to the Country Park entails a stiffish climb, but this is well rewarded by the splendour of the scenery. The Park's facilities more than repay the cost of admission, with the Tower providing unrivalled views. An easy descent back to Broadway sets the seal on a pleasant ramble.

Attractions   Broadway was for centuries a quiet farming village noted only for the summer residence of the Abbot of Pershore, which still stands on the Green. With the coming of the turnpike roads in the 17th century, several coaching inns sprang up. Horses were changed before the coaches faced the steep haul up Fish Hill and the place grew both in size and importance. An old milestone dating from this period can still be seen against the wall of the hotel bearing its name. Avoided by the railways, Broadway went through a quiet time until the coming of the motor car, when it was 'discovered' and became one of the most celebrated tourist attractions in the region.

     Bury End is said to have been the site of the original village of Broadway. The church of St. Eadburgh dates from Norman times and although it has lost its fine Elizabethan pulpit to the early Victorian church which replaced it, it is well worth a visit. The steps outside the churchyard are in fact a mounting block for the use of horse-riders.

     Broadway Tower stands at 1,024 feet above sea level and was built for the Countess of Coventry in 1798. The famous Victorian craftsman and poet William Morris lived here for a time and one of the three floors is given over to a display based on his life and work. The roof of the tower serves as a viewing platform.

     Although it is possible to pass through the park along the Cotswold Way footpath without paying, facilities on offer at a modest cost are ideal for children. They include an adventure playground, a ball games area, a gift shop (in the tower) and nature trails.

continued on page 12

Route 1

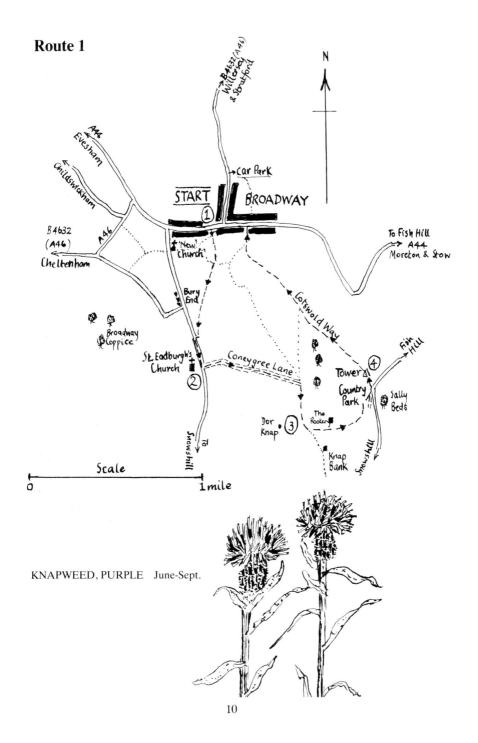

KNAPWEED, PURPLE   June-Sept.

10

Route 1

A Cotswold Corner

3¾ miles

START   *Broadway village, on A44 (Evesham — Stow-on-the-Wold road).* O.S. Sheet 150. GR 100375. *Large car park off Leamington Road.*

ROUTE

1. *From the car park, walk into the village. Cross the main street (A44). Turn right and in a short distance, opposite the Horse & Hound Inn, turn left along a footpath signposted 'Recreation Ground. To old Church 1 mile.' Keep a metal fence on the right. The 'new' church, St. Michael's, can be seen away to the right and Broadway Tower on the hilltop, left. Where the fence ends, cross a stile and keep straight on over a field to cross a stream. The clearly-defined path continues to a stile by a gate. Glorious views can be seen ahead. Cross another field and at the next stile, the old church can be glimpsed through the trees ahead. The footpath now draws near Bury End and the road to Snowshill, which it meets at Lybrook Farm. Turn left along the road to St. Eadburgh's Church.*

2. *Opposite the church is a track signposted 'Broadway Tower'. This is Coneygree Lane, difficult in wet conditions. Follow this track to a T-junction. At the T-junction at the top of the lane, turn right to pass through a gate. Climb the grassy track, passing a deer enclosure and a bungalow on the left and cross a stile.*

3. *Turn left along a track just before stone gateway pillars. Continue along this track to meet a road. Turn left along the road, climbing towards woodland. Nearing the summit, turn left through a gate into Broadway Tower Country Park. The footpath passes through another gate and bears right past buildings to a drive. Just beyond the admission kiosk, go left over a stile to the tower.*

4. *From the tower, the Cotswold Way footpath descends the slope in the direction of Broadway, which is reached after a mile or so of pleasant, easy walking. To return to the car park, either use the footpath opposite or turn left to the A46 junction (Leamington Road).*

ACCESS BY BUS
Broadway is connected to Evesham, Cheltenham and Winchcombe. (Castleways Coaches).

The descent back to Broadway is enriched in summer by a host of limestone-loving wild flowers, including scabious, knapweed, St. John's Wort, harebell and eyebright. Butterflies, too, are abundant in the sunshine. Skylarks and yellowhammers are in song from March until midsummer.

Refreshments There are plenty of refreshment facilities in Broadway. Alternatively, morning coffee, snacks and teas can be obtained at the Country Park.

BREDON HILL

Bredon Hill

Outline   Bredon's Norton ~ Woollas Hall ~ Bredon Hill ~ Kemerton-Westmancote ~ Bredon's Norton.

Summary   Bredon Hill is an outlier of the main Cotswold range and rises to 961 feet above sea level at its highest point. Like all high places, it demands its price of the walker in terms of effort, but the rewards are rich indeed. Fossils, prehistoric remains, wild life, glorious views - not to mention literary associations - all these are to be found in abundance. Selecting a walk to cover the best of Bredon is far from easy; 5 miles of this particular route must be covered before the pub is reached, so an early start is strongly recommended!

Attractions   'In summertime on Bredon
                                the bells they sound so clear'
wrote the poet A. E. Housman. Another poet, John Drinkwater, wrote of one of Bredon's villages:
                    'God laughed when he made Grafton,
                    That's under Bredon Hill.'
    Other celebrated writers, including John Moore and Fred Archer, have added their share of praise to that of the poets. It is hoped that a little of the magic these men found on Bredon Hill will convey itself to families making the long, hard climb to the top.
    The ascent may be tiring but there is plenty to see on the way. Approaching Woollas Hall, a field covered with overgrown anthills is worth looking out for, as is an area of rare wetland habitat, fenced off by the Nature Conservancy. Woollas Hall is a fine old house. It was rebuilt in 1611 and it is said that during the persecution of Roman Catholics it was used as a refuge by priests, who hid in the building's many concealed corners to avoid capture and death at the hands of the soldiers.
    Approaching the summit of the hill, keen eyes will spot fossilised shellfish embedded in fragments of limestone strewn along the way. These rocks date back about 150 million years, as do those of the nearby Cotswolds. For those more interested in modern technology, the row of radar detectors are worth noting, especially if the visibility is good enough to pick out the associated 'golf balls' on Defford airfield, five miles or so to the north-west across the Avon Valley.
    The tower on the summit of the hill may be somewhat unexceptional to look at but there is an odd story associated with it. According to local

continued on page 16

13

Route 2

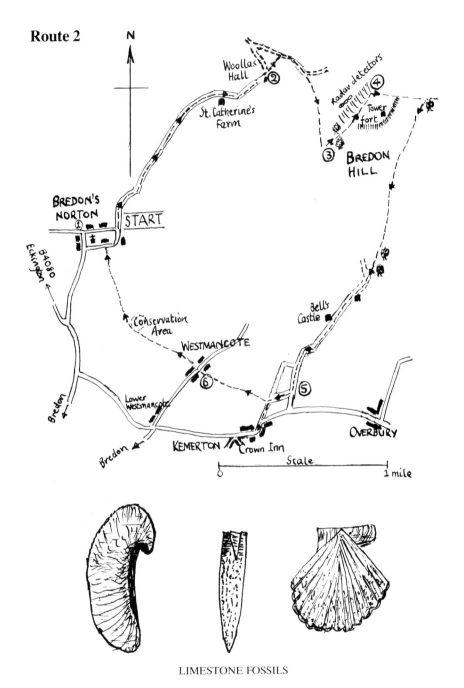

N

Woollas Hall ②

Radar detectors ④

Tower fort

③ BREDON HILL

St. Catherine's Farm

BREDON'S NORTON ①

START

B4080 Eckington

Bredon

Conservation Area

WESTMANCOTE ⑥

Bell's Castle

Lower Westmancote

⑤

Bredon

KEMERTON Crown Inn

OVERBURY

Scale

0   1 mile

LIMESTONE FOSSILS

14

Route 2

Bredon Hill

7½ miles

START *Bredon's Norton village, ½ mile east of B4080, 2 miles north of Bredon* (O.S. Sheet 150 GR 930390). *Park in village.*

ROUTE

1. *From the small circular island in the village, climb the lane by the telephone box. At a T-junction, turn left along a lane signposted 'No Through Road'. This lane soon bears right by a small wood and climbs between hedges. Cross a cattle grid and follow the private drive to St. Catherine's Farm. Keep on over cattle grids up to Woollas Hall.*

2. *Beyond the Hall grounds, do not follow the drive downhill to the left. Instead, keep straight on to the left of a wire fence to meet a track climbing uphill from the left. Follow this track uphill until it turns sharp left, at which point, cross a stile on the right by a gate into a field. Head diagonally left towards a wood, aiming for a large forked tree and keeping radar detectors on the left and with a tower also away to the left on the skyline. Go through a metal gate to the right of and in front of the tree to meet a rough track. Cross over and follow a grassy track climbing between two banks with woodland ahead. Climb over a gate in a stone wall to reach a woodland track.*

3. *You have now climbed over 200 metres. To reach the summit of Bredon Hill, turn left through the wood and, keeping the stone wall on the left, aim for the tower which marks the highest point of the ridge.*

4. *To continue the walk, keep on along the ridge with a wall on the left as far as a small wood. Bear right in front of the wood to follow another stone wall roughly at right angles to the first. A radio mast soon appears away to the left as the tower recedes to the right. Keep the stone wall on the left, passing the picturesque Lalu Farm away to the left and with views of the Cotswolds beyond. Ignore side-tracks, continuing to descend with the ever-present wall on the left, eventually passing an old quarry on the right, beyond which the route enters a wood through a handgate. Leave the wood and follow the descending track, which becomes metalled beyond farm buildings, and remains so down to Kemerton.*

5. *To continue the walk, turn right in the village along a lane by a house, King's Lea (Letter box in wall). At the T-junction ahead turn left by Laurel Cottage for the Crown Inn and the village. Retrace your steps to the T-junction, then take the footpath between houses on the left signposted to Westmancote.*

B

15

6. *At Westmancote, cross the street and take the signposted footpath to Bredon's Norton by passing through a farm gate and along a rubbled track (grassy later). A slight diversion is necessary to pass a small wetland conservation area. After crossing a footbridge, keep the field hedge on the right. Bredon's Norton Church soon appears ahead and is reached by continuing along the path to meet a road.*

ACCESS BY BUS
There is an infrequent service to Kemerton. (Evesham-Tewkesbury route, operated by Midland Red West).

---

tradition, its builder, a Mr. Parsons of Kemerton, constructed it to a height of exactly 39 feet so that its top raised the 961-feet summit to 1,000 feet.

But Bredon's most impressive feature is the vast prehistoric fort crowning the hilltop. We can imagine the violent struggles that went on between hostile tribes here long ago. Revived after a rest, lively children may wish to re-enact the turbulent past, while parents opt for communing with nature like the poets who found inspiration here.

Refreshments The Crown Inn, Kemerton. Bar luches. Children welcome.

CLEEVE PRIOR

Route 3
6¼ miles

Avon Valley and Cleeve Prior

Outline   Fish & Anchor, Offenham ~ Cleeve Prior ~ Cleeve Hill ~ Fish & Anchor.

Summary   This is an easy, pleasant ramble upstream along the right bank of the River Avon to the attractive village of Cleeve Prior, close to the Warwickshire border. From here, the route follows the long, low, wooded ridge known as Cleeve Hill, which provides good views of the Avon Valley and is rich in natural history.

Attractions   River-bank walking is seldom without interest, and this stretch of the so-called Warwickshire (or Shakespeare's) Avon offers plenty to see throughout the year. Like the rivers Nene and Welland, the Avon begins its life in Northamptonshire not far from the Civil War battlefield of Naseby. Flowing in a South-westerly direction towards the Severn, it picks its way past Rugby, Leamington Spa, Warwick and Stratford before we meet it here, and its size is therefore quite impressive.

River craft are a prominent feature of the walk. They range from brightly-painted traditional narrow-boats of the kind seen on canals to sleek sporty motor boats and spacious cabin cruisers. Anglers frequent the river bank in great numbers during the summer months, especially at weekends and bank holidays. They are chiefly members of works' angling clubs, often from the Birmingham area, and their fishing-places are spaced out and marked with numbered pegs. It is worth noting what an extensive range of equipment they bring with them to ensure that they are fully prepared for a long day by the waterside.

River banks are rich wildlife habitat and this one is no exception. A wide variety of water-loving plants can be seen along the first stretch of the walk, one of the most attractive being the Himalayan Balsam, a large plant with reddish stems and pink flowers, which has spread along British river banks in recent years. Three interesting poisonous plants can also be seen - deadly nightshade, hemlock and cuckoo pint.

The village of Cleeve Prior is full of interest. The main street comprises a rich mixture of building styles, including houses of stone, red brick and colour-washed brick. Some of the buildings bear datestones but these are not always easy to read. Talking of datestones, do not miss seeing the grave of Sara Charlett, who was buried in 1793 south of the church tower. The mason appears to have recorded her age as 309, but

continued on page 20

17

Route 3

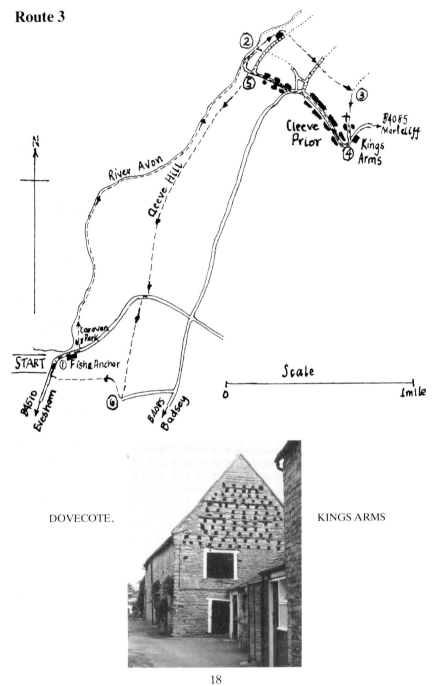

DOVECOTE,   KINGS ARMS

Route 3

Avon Valley and Cleeve Prior

6¼ miles

START *Fish & Anchor Inn, on the B4510, between Offenham and Cleeve Prior, 4 miles N.E. of Evesham. Park by the riverside near the Inn.* (O.S. Sheet 150, GR 067471).

ROUTE

1. *From the inn, walk along the road by the river towards Cleeve Prior as far as the entrance to a caravan park on the left. Follow the footpath signposted to Cleeve Prior through the park. Beyond the caravans, this path follows the river bank, passing a weir and cottages. Where the woodland on the right reaches the river bank, ignore a path marked with a 5 on the right and keep straight on to where the footpath joins a metalled track.*

2. *Where the metalled track turns off to the right, just before a liftbelt-holder, follow it for a short distance. Ignore the path signposted to the church. Instead, follow another path slightly to the left, which climbs through woods, bending to the right to pass a cottage on the right. At a crossroads of paths, continue straight on and over a second crossroads of paths to a T-junction of tracks. Go straight on over this, keeping a hedge on the right. Near the end of the field, go through a gap on the right and keep the hedge on the left in the next field to reach a stile.*

3. *Cross the stile and turn right to pass a pond on the right and cross a plank bridge and a stile. In the next field, aim for a horse chestnut tree slightly to the left of the church tower ahead. The old hall can now be seen on the left. Crossing a fence by the tree, enter the churchyard through a gap in the hedge, and leave through a metal handgate between two old stone buildings, where a pebbled path leads to the King's Arms Inn.*

4. *To continue the walk from the inn, turn along the village street (B4085). Leave this road along Mill Lane (signposted on the right). Continue past new houses and over the brow of the hill to a bridleway on the left signposted Littleton.*

5. *Follow this bridleway to a road (B4510). Turn right and follow the road for 50 metres to the signposted path on the left. Follow this to a junction of tracks.*

6. *At this junction, turn right and immediately right again to descend along a track between hedges which soon passes through open fields to reach the B4510 near the inn.*

Cleeve Prior is on the Birmingham-Redditch-Evesham route. (Midland Red West).

---

closer inspection reveals that having spaced the figures 3 and 9 too far apart, he inserted a circular flourish to bridge the gap!

The house martin emblem at the start of the bridleway over Cleeve Hill reminds us that we are crossing a reserve maintained by the Worcestershire Nature Conservation Trust. Watch out for yellowhammers and long-tailed tits and listen from early April onwards for the chiffchaff calling its name from the undergrowth.

Refreshments The King's Arms, Cleeve Prior. Bar food. Garden. Children welcome.

The Fish and Anchor, Offenham. Hot and cold bar snacks. Children welcome.

Nearby attraction: Middle Littleton tithe barn (National Trust). A fine 14th-century building recently restored. 136 feet long and roofed with Cotswold stone tiles.

PERSHORE ABBEY

Pershore & Tyddesley Wood

Outline   Pershore (Abbey) ~ Old & New Bridge ~ Tyddesley Wood ~ Pershore.

Summary   Pershore is the only town included in the walking itineraries of this book, a distinction it owes to its outstanding interest and charm. It is but a short walk from the town centre to the two bridges - one old, one new - that span the River Avon, and there follows an interesting riverside walk to Tyddesley Woods, a remnant of ancient woodland rich in plant, insect and bird life. There is no pub or similar facility along the route, but refreshments are readily obtainable in Pershore at the end of this easy walk.

Attractions   Pershore is a Georgian town, built largely during the 17th and 18th centuries and such is its quality and character that it is one of only 51 English towns designated as being of major historical importance and thus worthy of special conservation measures. It is well worth lingering in the handsome streets, taking in the atmosphere of a bygone age and imagining the horse-drawn coaches rumbling through the many arched entrances to the inns and other noble buildings.

The abbey, with its 14th century tower, was once a much larger building until the monasteries were destroyed by order of King Henry VIII. What remains was saved by the townspeople for use as their church. The park surrounding the abbey is ideal for play and picnics.

The old bridge over the River Avon also dates from the 14th century and is said to have been built by the monks. The central span was blown up by Royalist soldiers during the Civil War in an attempt to halt the advance of Cromwell's forces.

Pershore boasts the only college of further education devoted entirely to horticulture. The town also gave its name to two plums, the Pershore Egg and the Pershore Purple.

After having wriggled its way through Evesham, the River Avon has gained considerably in width since we encountered it on the previous walk. It will be a river of even greater consequence by the time it flows past Eckington and Bredon to meet the Severn at Tewkesbury, of course, but the walk to Tyddesley Wood along the river bank cannot fail to delight young and old alike. Boats, anglers, plant, bird and insect life ensures that every step brings new interest. Of the waterside flowers, the

continued on page 24

Route 4

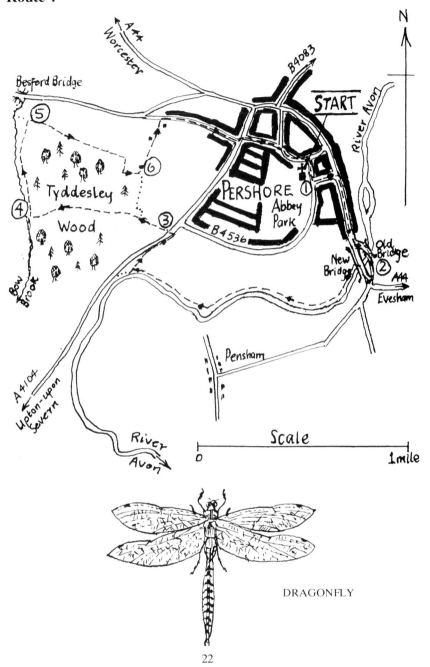

N

Worcester A44

Besford Bridge

B4083

START

River Avon

⑤

Tyddesley

⑥

PERSHORE

Abbey Park

①

④

Wood

③

B4536

Bow Brook

Old Bridge

New Bridge

②

A44

Evesham

A4104 Upton-upon Severn

Pensham

River Avon

Scale

0   1mile

DRAGONFLY

22

Route 4
Pershore and Tyddesley Wood   5 miles

START   *In the town of Pershore, at the west end of Broad Street, near the Abbey* (O.S. Sheet 150, GR 948458). *Limited parking nearby.*

ROUTE
1. *Walk along Broad Street and turn right down High Street (A44). The old town bridge is on the left hand side of the road and can be reached by a slip road.*

2. *From the old bridge, cross the A44 and the new bridge and take the footpath signposted Tyddesley Wood. The path keeps to the north (right hand) bank of the River Avon for about 1½ miles before leaving it just beyond a wooden footbridge to pass through a stile and join a road (The A4104). Turn right and walk along the verge for a short distance before crossing at a market garden to follow a bridleway sign up a lane.*

3. *At the top of the lane, go through a gate by a charming black-and-white thatched cottage and enter a field. Ignore a stile on the right. Instead, keep the hedge on the right and cross two stiles, 20 metres apart, and approach Tyddesley Wood with a fence lined by damson trees on the left. Enter the wood (noting the Worcestershire Nature Conservation Trust sign) and follow the bridleway straight ahead. At the extremity of the right-hand woodland, just before the track dips (with views of open country ahead), watch for a stile on the right.*

4. *Cross this stile and turn right to follow the outer edge of the wood along the margin of a field. Another stile is reached at the end of the wood.*

5. *Cross this stile, but instead of crossing another leading downhill, turn right over a ditch to follow the left-hand path along the inner edge of the wood to a clearing with a 'Number 1' marker post for a nature trail and a gate on the left. A diversion can be made here if so desired. Otherwise, keep straight on, crossing a stile alongside the gate and keeping the woodland edge to the right. Cross 2 stiles and climb the slope to the end of the wood. Pershore Abbey is now visible ahead. Follow the fence round to the left and watch for a footbridge 30 metres to the left of the corner of the field. Instead of crossing the bridge, however, keep on round the edge of the field to reach a grassy track between some derelict buildings.*

6. *From the start of the track, keep straight on, with views of the Abbey on the right. Pass a large green shed on the left and a barn on the right to meet a road. Turn right and descend back into Pershore by turning left*

and immediately right at a T-junction. The Abbey comes into view on the right ahead.

ACCESS BY BUS

Pershore is connected by bus with Worcester and Evesham. (Midland Red West)

----

tall, elegant purple loosestrife is especially memorable, while among the insects, giant dragonflies abound in the summer sunshine.

Tyddesley Wood is a nature lover's paradise. The wide rides attract some of our loveliest butterflies, including the brimstone, the comma, and the white admiral, while throughout spring and summer, such appealing wild flowers as yellowwort, centaury and fleabane, brighten the way. The wood is scheduled as a nature reserve and is managed by the Worcestershire Nature Conservation Trust.

Refreshments Obtainable in Pershore.

LOCK NEAR TARDEBIGGE

The Worcester and Birmingham Canal

Outline   Tardebigge Church ~ Queen's Head Inn, Stoke Pound ~ Dusthouse Lane ~ Grimley Lane ~ Tardebigge Church.

Summary   Walking along canal towpaths is both easy and full of interest. There is no problem with gradients, the route is never in doubt, and this enables every member of the party to give undivided attention to the unique atmosphere of the 'cut'. The leisurely tempo, too, has its own special appeal - so much so that I suspect that many walkers will be content to retrace their steps from the Queen's Head, rather than part company with the towpath for the return route. Those who do 'complete the course' should enjoy the short diversion from the canal however, especially any railway enthusiasts. In any case, the last stage of the walk entails retracing the route from the reservoir to Tardebigge Church.

Attractions   Few hamlets can boast such a proud claim to fame as tiny Tardebigge. St. Bartholomew's Church, perched on its hill, was built in 1777 and its 135-foot spire is a landmark for miles around. Together with the nearby school and rectory, it makes an attractive group. But it was some 40 years after the church was built that Tardebigge's name became famous. In 1815, the Worcester-to-Birmingham canal was finally opened after a quarter of a century of difficult construction, including the building of the huge flight of locks we see today. These locks carry the waterway over 200 feet up the hillside in 2½ miles to the mouth of the Tardebigge tunnel and were constructed by gangs of navvies (short for navigators) who moved thousands of tons of earth with their spades and wheelbarrows.

Today, this canal is still in use, although the trading narrow boats of bygone times have been replaced by pleasure craft. Climbing or descending the flight of locks means a busy time for the crews, who have to open the lock gates with special windlasses before their boats can pass through.

Two features connected with the supply of water for this stretch of the canal are of special interest. One is the former pumping station, which after lying derelict for many years, has now been converted into a restaurant. The other is Tardebigge Reservoir, built to supply water to replace that lost by the constant opening and closing of the lock gates.

This reservoir is now a haven for wild life, especially birds, and enthusiasts should come equipped with binoculars. Among the species

continued on page 28

Route 5

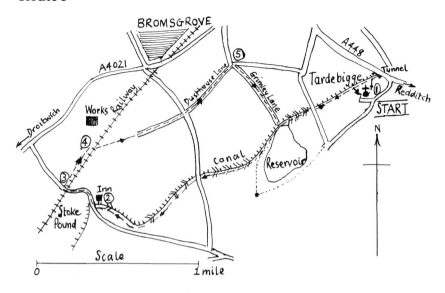

TARDEBIGGE RESERVOIR

Route 5

The Worcester and Birmingham Canal 6 miles

START   *Tardebigge Church. This prominent landmark stands ¼ mile south of the A418, midway between Bromsgrove and Redditch. (O.S. Sheet 139. GR 996692). Park near the church.*

ROUTE

1. *At the entrance to the churchyard, turn right through a kissing gate and follow the path down to the canal. After seeing the mouth of the Tardebigge Tunnel, turn left along the towpath. The route follows the towpath for about 2½ miles as far as the bridge by the Queen's Head Inn.*

2. *From the bridge (or the inn), turn right along the road to pass a nursery (on the left) and a pumping station (on the right). Keep straight on as far as a railway bridge.*

3. *Immediately beyond the bridge, climb up the grassy bank on the right to reach a metalled path running straight alongside the railway. Follow this path until it bends to the left at a lamp standard.*

4. *Climb the steps on the right and* **cross this busy main-line track with great care.** *In the field, turn left to follow the edge parallel to the railway. At the end of the field, bear right along the hedge to a wide opening. Turn through this gap, keeping to the right of a hedge and proceed through a gate and into a lane. Keep straight on along this lane (Dusthouse Lane) to the second junction, with Walnut Lane on the left and Grimley Lane on the right.*

5. *Turn right to climb Grimley Lane, passing the entrance to Grimley Hall drive. From the summit, the land dips down to the canal. Cross the bridge to re-join the towpath alongside Tardebigge Reservoir and turn left to retrace steps back to Tardebigge Church, which can be reached from the towpath by a signposted path alongside the lock-keeper's cottage.*

GREAT CRESTED GREBE,
BROWN AND BUFF   48cm

27

present throughout the year are mallard, coot, moorhen, great crested grebe and Canada goose, all of which breed in the reedy margins of the reservoir.

For those deciding to complete the full route, the stretch of walking away from the canal is over footpaths and along minor roads, and provides a glimpse of the pleasant countryside through which the great feat of canal engineering was constructed.

Refreshments The Queen's Head, Stoke Pound. Restaurant. Children welcome.

FORD, DOWLES BROOK

Wyre Forest

Outline   Far Forest ~ Callow Hill ~ Forest walk ~ Dowles Brook ford ~ Wimperhill Wood ~ Far Forest.

Summary   The Wyre Forest is a fascinating remnant of one of the vast tracts of wildwood that once covered much of Midland England. Many families discover something of its delights as a result of a visit to the Forestry Commission's centre at Callow Bank. For those who prefer to 'go it alone', rather than keep to the well-trodden paths, there are plenty of tempting alternatives, as this varied and fairly straightforward route shows.

Attractions   The very word 'forest' conjures up a host of romantic impressions in young and not-so-young alike. Indeed, the name of the somewhat unremarkable village of Far Forest, near which this walk begins, appealed so much to the region's novelist, Francis Brett Young, that he used it as the title of one of his works. Although what remains of the forest is dissected by roads and encroached upon by villages and scattered farms and houses, it retains much of its atmosphere of remoteness and mystery. In fact, with the abandoning of its coal and iron workings and the closure of the railway which once passes through it, the forest seems to have closed in and returned to its former pre-industrial state.

The Dowles Brook provides the forest with much of its charm. Fed by its tributary streams, the Baveney and Man brooks, the Dowles Brook flows eastwards through the trees to meet the Severn near Bewdley. It is said that its name means dark, or black even, but this description bears little relation to the water, the purity of which attracts three of our most colourful water-birds - the grey wagtail, the dipper and the kingfisher.

The ford across the Dowles Brook (4 on the Map) is an ideal spot for children to paddle and enjoy water-play.

In addition to water-birds, a wide range of woodland species are present, including tits (blue, great, coal, long-tailed and marsh), goldcrests, treecreepers and woodpeckers. Keen eyes will detect deer-prints in the mud. The insect population - dragonflies, butterflies, moths and beetles - is extensive, while wood ants scuttle backwards and forwards, carrying twigs far larger than themselves to further extend nests already a metre or so high.

continued on page 32

29

Route 6

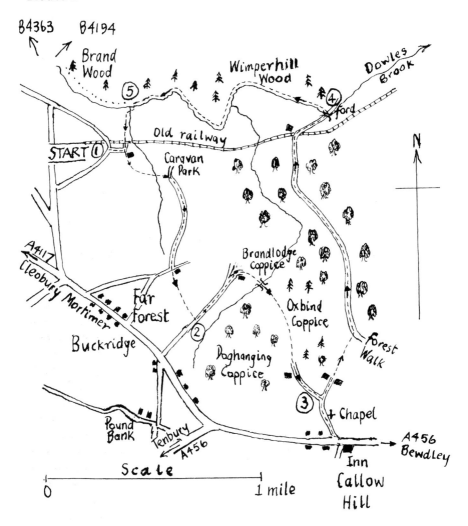

Scale

0   1 mile

Route 6

Wyre Forest

5½ miles

START   *About halfway between Bewdley and Cleobury Mortimer on the A4117 is the village of Far Forest. Take the minor road north from Far Forest signposted Wyre Forest. After about half a mile turn right at Triangle Farm along a minor road. Continue to where a forest approach lane joins on the right. Park on the grass verge near the lane.* (O.S. Sheet 138, GR 727758).

ROUTE

1. *Walk down the steep lane under the trees. At a left hand bend, take the path to the right of a cottage called The Newells. Cross a stream and bear left to enter woodland. Climb a slope to reach a lane near the entrance to a caravan park. Turn right, and at a junction, fork right along a minor road. In about half a mile, at a T-junction, cross a stile directly opposite and keep a hedge on the left across a field. Continue along a grassy path to a lane.*

2. *Turn left and at a fork, bear right by a bungalow. Follow the woodland path along the side of a bungalow garden (Brantwood). Keep on a descending path which bears to the right to cross a stream by a plank bridge to a stile. Enter woodland (Oxbind Coppice) and climb steadily to the top of the slope. Ignore a descending track on the right. Instead, keep straight on along a grassy track between fields, passing a farm on the right by a stile alongside a gate. Follow the lane to a T-junction.*

3. *Turn right and keep straight on for the Royal Forester Inn (Across the road and a short distance to the left). To continue the walk retrace your steps, passing the T-junction, then follow the rough path through a farmyard and into a wood. Keep straight on to meet the wide forest walk. Turn left along this. Ignore side-turns and keep straight on to a junction of forest paths. Ignore the forest walks sign on the right. Instead, keep straight on for about a mile down the wide path, passing Park House on the left, to cross a bridge with a ford to the right.*

4. *From the bridge, turn left along the bridleway, with a stream (Dowles Brook) on the left and conifer woodland on the right.*

5. *Where the track climbs and bends sharply to the right, bear left across the brook by the footbridge below. Cross another footbridge and climb a path to join a lane. Pass a cottage, a dismantled railway bridge and The Newells and climb up to the road and your car.*

Far Forest is on the Birmingham-Kidderminster-Hereford route. (Midland Red West)

Last, but by no means least, the forest trees deserve special mention. Many are very old - one gnarled and ancient oak is said to have a girth measuring 23½ feet. The native hardwoods - oak, beech, birch, ash, hazel - are supplemented by more recent plantings of softwood conifers, including larch, spruce and Douglas fir, reminding us that forestry, like all other forms of land-use, has an economic, as well as a scenic value.

Refreshments The Royal Forester Inn, Callow Hill. Lunches and snacks, Family room. Garden. Children welcome.

LOCK-KEEPER'S HOUSE, SALWARPE

Route 7

Salwarpe Valley and Droitwich Canal

Outline   Salwarpe village ~ Droitwich Canal ~ Mildenham Mill ~ Bowling Green Inn ~ Salwarpe village.

Summary   In contrast to Route 5, the greater part of which is along the towpath of a working canal, this walk is routed for about half of its length along a disused waterway. Instead of the lively and colourful sight of narrow boats and other vessels negotiating the locks, the walk traces what remains of a long abandoned trade route and ends with a stretch of pleasant, easy walking on minor roads and footpaths in the attractive Salwarpe Valley.

Attractions   Derelict canals have their own distinctive appeal. Their original attractions - brightly-painted boats, well-maintained lock-gates, tidy towpaths - have long since gone, but years of neglect have given them a new kind of fascination that many historians, naturalists, ramblers - and families, too - find irresistible.

The Droitwich Canal opened in 1771 and was constructed to develop the salt trade, for which the town of Droitwich had been famous for centuries. Its building was supervised by James Brindley, the celebrated self-taught engineer who had been responsible for the first great navigation, as canals were then called, in Lancashire. Its length was short - only 6¾ miles - but as the first efficient trade-link between Droitwich, Bristol (via the River Severn) and later Birmingham (via the Worcester and Birmingham canal), it was a busy and prosperous waterway until growing competition from the railways finally led to its abandonment just before the Second World War.

Like many other derelict canals, this one has attracted the attention of enthusiasts bent on restoring it to its original navigable state. There is evidence of their efforts early on the walk in the form of new lock-gates with a recently renovated lock-keeper's cottage alongside.

Chidren may well prefer discovering traces of the canal's history, rather than admiring the restorer's efforts, however, and there is plenty of evidence for the young industrial archaeologist to search for. Close inspection of the locks (easier than on a working canal) reveals overflow openings and ground paddles, while nearby can be seen lengths of old narrowgauge rail and rusting side-tipping trucks.

Naturalists in the family, meanwhile, will be fully absorbed in studying the wild life that has colonised this disused waterway. Water-

continued on page 36

Route 7

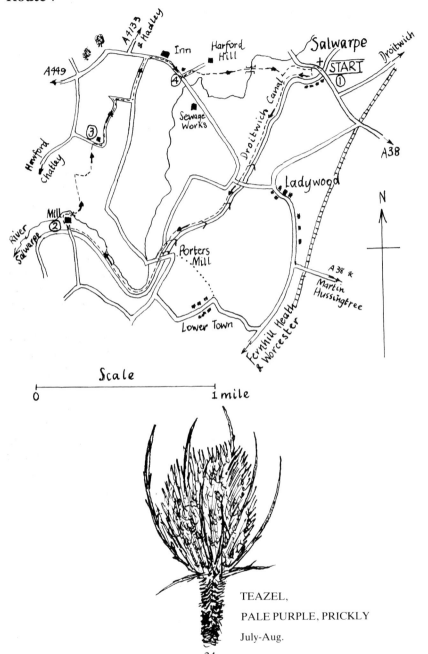

Scale
0   1 mile

TEAZEL,
PALE PURPLE, PRICKLY
July-Aug.

34

Route 7

Salwarpe Valley & Droitwich Canal   4½ miles

START *Salwarpe village, approximately 1 mile south-west of Droitwich. Approached by minor road from A38, ¼ mile south of the junction with the B4090. Park by the church. (O.S. Sheet 150, GR 875621).*

ROUTE

1. *Walk past the church along the lane and, at a signpost, cross over a stile on the left to follow a footpath. In 40 metres, cross another stile, also on the left. Climb the bank to the canal towpath and turn right. In about a mile, after passing a lock, cross a road by a bridge and return to the towpath. At the next road, turn left parallel to the canal and soon, at a T-junction, turn left to rejoin the towpath. Another mile or so of towpath-walking follows to the next bridge, where the walk leaves the canal at Mildenham Mill.*

2. *Immediately before the bridge and the gateway to the mill, turn sharp right through a metal gate to follow a footpath parallel to the canal towpath. This path, which can be muddy, bends to the left to cross a metal bridge. Over the bridge, bear left and head for the first of two metal handgates at either end of another bridge. Climb the bank ahead to pass through a gate (fitted with a special catch for horseriders) and keep straight on. Soon the path veers to the right between hedges with a pylon ahead. At a T-junction of paths, turn left and keep straight on to meet a road.*

3. *About a mile of minor-road walking now follows. Turn right and pass a black-and-white farmhouse. At a crossroads, turn left. Ignore a footpath on the right. Instead, keep straight on to a T-junction. Turn right (Ladywood on signpost). The Hadley Bowling Green Inn is soon reached on the left. From the inn, keep on in the same direction as before and at the foot of the slope, watch for a footpath signposted 'Salwarpe ¾' on the left by a house.*

4. *Follow this path along the track until another signpost indicates a deviation to the right. This entails dipping down the bank to a barbed-wire fence and keeping this on the right as far as a stile. (This section of the walk can be somewhat overgrown in summer). Cross the stile and climb the bank ahead, aiming slightly to the left. Salwarpe Church comes into view at the top. Aim for the church tower, crossing the River Salwarpe by a metal bridge. Keep straight on with a fence on the left. Follow the fence round to the right to a stile at the corner of the field.*

Descend the bank half-left to cross a bridge and climb to the right, passing the second stile (to the canal) crossed earlier, to reach the lane to the church by the first stile encountered at the start of the walk.

---

loving plants, such as reeds, reed-mace and great willowherb grow abundantly along damp stretches, while teazel, burdock, St. John's wort, bartsia, and a host of other wild flowers splash their colourful mantle along the overgrown margins elsewhere.

From May to August, skulking little sedge warblers rattle out their song from this dense cover. Moorhens and mallard breed in the safety of the low vegetation, while sharp-eyed spotters missing out on seeing a kingfisher by the canal can still make amends by catching a fleeting glimpse of this splendid bird skimming along the nearby river Salwarpe, as I was fortunate enough to do one August afternoon.

Nearby attractions: Hawford dovecote, 3 miles S.W. of Salwarpe (National Trust).

Refreshments Hadley Bowling Green Inn. Snacks and lunches. Garden. Children welcome.

THE HUNDRED HOUSE HOTEL

36

Route 8

(plus optional 1¼ miles circular to Abberley Village)

Abberley Hill

Outline Wynniates Way ~ Abberley Hill ~ Hundred House Hotel ~ Abberley Hall ~ Wynniates Way (optional: Abberley Village).

Summary The wooded hills of Worcestershire make delightful walking for family parties. While never exactly precipitous, these hill-walks nevertheless give children a sense of achievement and provide adults with rewarding views of a countryside whose subtle charms are far too often overlooked. The ascent to the 930-foot summit of Abberley Hill is tackled at the beginning of this walk, when everybody is fresh, and although the terrain remains undulating throughout, it is reassuring to know that the hardest section of the route has been left behind!

Attractions The scramble up to the concrete triangulation pillar near the start of the walk may well prompt children to want to know something of the way in which the Ordnance Survey puts our countryside on the map. Given clear visibility, they will being to understand why this hilltop vantage point was chosen as a survey site, for the view is extensive.

Prominent to the south-west is the clock tower known as Jones' Folly, erected just over a century ago by the eccentric squire of Abberley for the sole purpose, according to local belief, of looking down on his wealthy and influential neighbour at nearby Great Witley Court! Away to the south rises Woodbury Hill, upon which Iron-Age people constructed a hill-fort and where, in 1402, the Welsh leader Owen Glendower encamped with his army during his campaign against King Henry IV. Over two centuries later, Woodbury yet again provided the lofty setting for a minor historical event. In 1645, an armed gathering of Worcestershire people - farmers, tradesmen and ordinary villagers - declared their contempt and defiance of the armies - both Royalist and Roundhead - that had robbed, bullied and terrorised them throughout the Civil War - a bold new assertion of the old saying 'A plague on both your houses!'

Historical associations are thick on the ground in this corner of Worcestershire. As its distinctive sign suggests, the Georgian Hundred House Hotel boasts an out-of-the-ordinary past, having once served as a coroner's court - surely one for the record books.

Like the other woodland walks in this book, this one provides plenty of interest for nature lovers. Whatever the time of year, tree-feeding and

continued on page 40

Route 8

Scale

0   1 mile

38

Route 8

Abberley Hill
2½ miles

(plus optional 1¼ miles circular to Abberley village)

START   *Wynniates Way, a minor road climbing northwards from the A443, just to the east of its junction with the B4202, and a mile north-west of Great Witley. Limited parking on the verge just beyond the brow of the hill. (O.S. Sheet 150, GR 750674).*

ROUTE

1. *Walk back to the brow of the hill and cross the stile signposted 'Public Footpath Redmarley' on the left. The path climbs through woodland, curving to the right at first before bending to the left to reach a triangulation pillar at 930 feet above sea level. From the pillar, keep on along the ridge with a metal fence on the right. The path narrows after the fence ends but keep on straight ahead as far as a wedge-shaped marker post.*

2. *From the post, leave the ridge path, turning right to descend through the woods. On reaching a line of old fence posts, keep as close as possible to them. As the ground levels out, the path bears to the right, passes a manhole cover near a patch of marshy ground, skirts a fallen tree and turns left at a T-junction to leave the woodland at a stile. Cross a field, keeping a fence on the left. (There is a good view of the clock tower on the right). Cross another stile about 20 metres down from the corner. In the next field, keep the hedge on the left to meet a road (the A443) at the Hundred House Hotel.*

3. *From the Hotel, turn right along the A443. 50 metres past its junction with the B4203 cross the road to reach the entrance to a track to the right of a white cottage.*

4. *Follow this track, keeping left at a fork to pass a small pool on the right. The track winds uphill through woodland, passing a walled garden on the left to a T-junction. Turn right, climbing through parkland to reach Abberley Hall (now a school). Follow the outside of the buildings to reach a junction of 5 ways.*

5. *Take the rough, stony rising path, **not** the main drive ahead, along which a public footpath sign points. Pass a deer farm on the left and the clock tower behind the trees on the right and descend to a road (the A443). Cross with care and walk up Wynniates Way, directly opposite, back to the car.*

EXTENDING THE ROUTE

Those families wishing to visit Abberley Village (as distinct from Abberley) to see the tiny restored Norman church of St. Michael can do so by following the roads and footpaths (dotted lines) shown on the sketch map.

ACCESS BY BUS

An infrequent service links Great Witley with Worcester. (Midland Red West)

———

nesting birds can be studied at close quarters. These include such small species as tits and treecreepers and larger birds such as jays and woodpeckers. Woodland flowers add their share of interest, while in autumn, fungi of many kinds thrive on decaying wood.

Neaby attractions. Greaty Witley Court and Church   The former a ruin, having been burnt down in 1937, the latter a striking example of 18th century baroque architecture within an uninspiring exterior often likened to a warehouse!

Refreshments   Hundred House Hotel, Great Witley. Snacks and lunches. Restaurant. Children welcome.

WORCESTERSHIRE BEACON FROM NORTH HILL

40

The Malvern Hills - North

Outline   Upper Wyche ~ Worcestershire Beacon ~ North Hill ~ St. Ann's Well ~ Upper Wyche.

Summary   Bracing hill-walking, magnificent views, a sense of achievement - this short walk offers all these rewards to the well-shod, wisely-clad family who, having pitted themselves successfully against less-challenging terrain, now wish to tackle the nearest thing to mountain-climbing east of the Black Mountains. And although at the peak of the holiday season this splendid hill-walk suffers the pressures of over-use, it is still possible to undertake the climb in midweek or at off-season times and enjoy something of the isolation that enhances the experience for young and not-so-young alike.

Attractions   Who can fail to experience a thrill on first seeing the Malverns rise in bluish-purple majesty from the Midlands Plain? And as we ascend to the 1,395-feet summit of the Worcestershire Beacon, we stand upon some of the oldest rocks in the country, many of which were created by volcanic action ages before the simplest of life-forms evolved.

These rocks may not contain fossils, but children will be able to see, with the help of a hand-lens, the crystals of mica, felspar and quartz, some of the minerals which are rain-resistant and helped create the wells of pure water for which Malvern is noted. At St. Ann's Well, the spa water can be seen and sampled, although few young people tasting it will be impressed by its flavour.

The topograph on the Beacon is, by contrast, a much more popular attraction. It is said that no less than 14 counties can be seen from this point on a clear day, although most children will be content to identify the towers of the 3 cathedrals - Worcester, Hereford and Gloucester - with the aid of binoculars.

Another striking experience unique to the Malverns - and to North Hill in particular - is the effect of looking down on Great Malvern. Children are impressed by the way in which the cacophony of everyday sounds rise with uncanny clarity to the 1,208-feet summit as the little town throbs with activity below.

Next to binoculars, perhaps the most popular item of extra equipment on these slopes is a kite. There can be few better places to indulge in this hobby (Great Malvern, incidentally, has its own kite shop). But for those content to enjoy watching wild life, the hovering

continued on page 44

41

Route 9

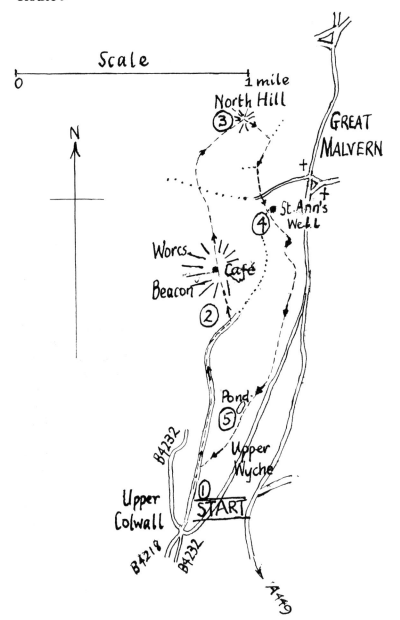

Route 9

The Malvern Hills - North

3¾ miles

START *Upper Wyche, Great Malvern, near the junction of the B4218 and the B4232. (Also junction of Walwyn Road, West Malvern Road and Beacon Road). The walk starts from the car park on Beacon Road. (O.S. Sheet 150. GR 770440).*

ROUTE

1. *From the car park, take the metalled path which eventually climbs to the Worcestershire Beacon. Notice the low cylindrical direction-indicator, marked 'Gold mine', on the right. This is the place at which the return route joins the path. The adventurous may wish to cut corners by leaving the main path. Whatever the exact route taken, the obvious destination is the summit of the Worcestershire Beacon, upon which stands a monument and a cafe.*

2. *From the summit, descend along the obvious northern path to pass another direction-indicator. For North Hill, follow the steep grassy path ahead where the main path bends sharply to the right.*

3. *North Hill, though not so high as the Worcestershire Beacon (1208 feet compared with 1395 feet), is reached after a steep climb. The summit is marked by a small cairn of stones. To descend to St. Ann's Well, turn right in the direction of Great Malvern, spread out below, and, heading in the direction of the prominent pinnacled tower of the Priory Church, descend over the rough ground to reach a lower level path. Turn right, and where it bends sharply to the right by a bench, descend straight on through the bracken, aiming in the direction of a track climbing to a small building ahead (St. Ann's Well). At the foot of this steep slope (slippery after rain), cross a road and follow the red-surfaced track which climbs, then dips, to St. Ann's Well.*

4. *From St. Ann's Well, follow the path signposted Wyche Road. (The sign is in the wall under a tree). Where the path dips to meet a road, climb another path on the right signposted Wyche Cutting. This path leads to a clearing with a pond on the right.*

5. *Leaving the clearing, take the right-hand path and keep to the right. This path climbs steadily. At the top, where the path is flanked by a wall on the left, ignore a sharp turn to the right. Instead, keep straight on to arrive at the 'Gold mine' direction-indicator passed earlier. Turn left down the track to the car park.*

43

A good bus service connects Great Malvern with Worcester. (Midland Red West).

---

kestrel hanging in the wind leaves even the finest kite behind in its use of the air currents. Of the smaller birds, meadow pipits are the most common species on the exposed slopes, with white-rumped wheatears as companions from late March until early autumn.

Butterfly enthusiasts should not miss examining the margins of the quarry pond near the end of the walk. A profusion of buddleia bushes grow here and on sunny days the purple blossom is alive with peacocks, red admirals and small tortoiseshells.

Refreshments   There is a cafe on Worcestershire Beacon and another at St. Ann's Well.

GIANT'S CAVE

44

The Malvern Hills - South
Herefordshire Beacon & Castlemorton Common

Outline   Beacon car park ~ British Camp ~ Giant's Cave ~ Castlemorton Common ~ Underhill Farm ~ Beacon car park.

Summary   This is a walk of contrasts. Beginning with the stiff climb from the car park up to the British Camp on Herefordshire Beacon, the route then follows the scenic ridge path southwards before making the steep descent down to Castlemorton Common, an extensive area of open unfenced heath rich in natural history interest. Another testing climb up to the reservoir on the flank of the Beacon then follows before the walk concludes with an easy level stretch back to the car park.

Attractions   Of all the 26 miles of footpaths spreading out over the Malvern Hills, none is more popular than that scaling the British Camp. Yet even now, with concrete paths and a constant tide of visitors, that feeling of awe remains, and it is easy to understand why John Masefield, born at nearby Ledbury and later to become Poet Laureate, wrote many years ago of the 'vastness, of roughness, and of something vast, rough and uncanny with a life of its own, like itself everlasting and strange; not inhuman, but not human.'

For the British Camp, hacked out of this great hill by Iron Age men, covers 45 acres and it has been estimated that 20,000 people could be gathered within its 1¾-mile perimeter. Legend has it that the valiant British king Caractacus resisted the Romans here, before his betrayal at Caer Caradoc - all stirring stuff for children as they scramble over the slopes.

Centuries later, the so-called Red Earl's Dyke was cut into the Beacon, moulding yet further the contours of the great hill. As the entire area was part of a vast royal hunting forest however, it was preserved from the piecemeal exploitation that affected much of the country and as a result we can enjoy its wildness today.

Castlemorton Common, as its name suggests, is unenclosed grazing land sheltering under the Malvern ridge, providing ideal conditions not only for sheep but also for many forms of wild life - and for those wishing to observe them. The mixed scrub and woodland habitat where hill and common meet is ideal for birdwatching during spring and early summer. Whitethroats and tree pipits find suitable breeding conditions here, cuckoos are usually plentiful, and keen ears may detect the rapid trilling of a wood warbler coming from the dense cover.

continued on page 48

45

Route 10

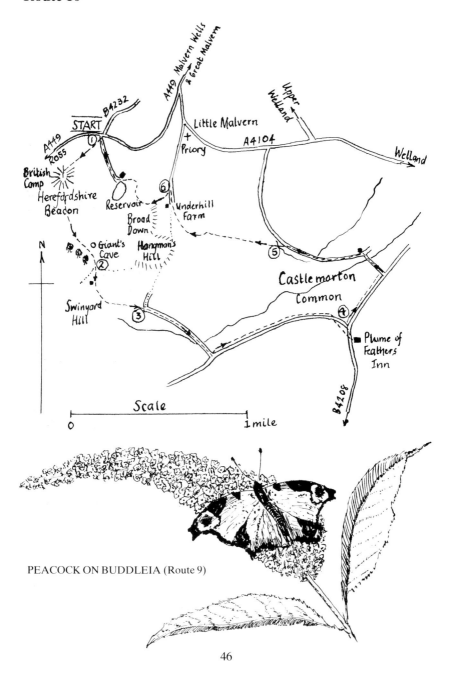

PEACOCK ON BUDDLEIA (Route 9)

Route 10

The Malvern Hills - South

5 miles

Herefordshire Beacon and Castlemorton Common

START   *About four miles south of Great Malvern, where the A449 to Ledbury is joined by the B4232. Park at the car park near the British Camp.* (O.S. Sheet 150. GR 763404).

ROUTE

1. *From the car park, follow the metalled path which climbs steeply to the summit of the Herefordshire Beacon, on which the vast prehistoric earthworks can be clearly seen. From the summit, keep straight on along the ridge, with an obelisk (The Somers Monument) away to the right ahead. Another metalled path now descends to a cylindrical signpost. Take the route indicating Giant's Cave (also known as Clutter's Cave). Beyond the cave, with the obelisk now straight ahead, descend through trees to a 3-pronged fork of paths. (A signpost in the wall indicates Hangman's Hill and Broad Down to the left).*

2. *From this point, take the middle (grassy) path and descend through the bracken to pass a cottage on the right. (This path can be wet after heavy rain). Castlemorton Common soon comes into view ahead. At a fork in the path near a double power pole, keep to the right to reach a track winding in from the left.*

3. *Follow this track to the right and on to Castlemorton Common. The Cotswolds lie straight ahead and Bredon Hill is away to the left. At a crossroads, turn left along the roadside. Welland Church lies ahead. A T-junction with a bus-stop soon comes into view. Those wishing to call for refreshment at the 'Plume of Feathers' Inn should turn off to the right just before the junction, following a narrow path and aiming slightly to the right of a phone box. The inn lies straight across the B4208.*

4. *To resume the walk at the T-junction, turn left along the roadside with Welland Church ahead. Take the next minor road on the left. The Malverns now loom straight ahead. Cross a stream (there is an excellent picnic spot under the trees on the right). In 100 metres or so, turn left at a cottage, cross a bridge, and follow a metalled road. Instead of passing through a gate, cross a single-plank bridge on the left.*

5. *From the bridge follow the path (stony at first), towards the hills. This path eventually veers to the right between trees and becomes a narrow footpath ending at a handgate, where it joins the track to Underhill Farm, now visible ahead. Pass the farm and at the top of the slope, near a yew tree, reach a stile by a gate on the left.*

6. *Cross the stile and make for the left-hand of 2 gates to enter the woodland ahead, passing a giant lime tree on the way. Climb through the trees to meet a path. Turn right along it and climb the steep slope by the reservoir to reach the car park.*

ACCESS BY BUS

A good bus service connects Great Malvern with Worcester. (Midland Red West)

Prickly yellow-blossomed gorse is the predominant plant of the dry areas of the common. It offers secure nestsites to linnets and is festooned with cobwebs, which show up strikingly in misty or frosty conditions. The damp patches of the common attract curlews and are rich in plant life, as those families equipped with a suitable book will discover. Rushes, sedges, marsh speedwell and bog stitchwort are examples of plants to watch out for.

Giant puffballs are a feature of the common in late summer. Notice the heather on the bank of the reservoir on the last stage of the walk.

Refreshments Plume of Feathers Inn, Castlemorton Common. Snacks and meals. Family facilities. Garden.
Malvern Hills Hotel, Herefordshire Beacon. Lunches.

ORCHARD NEAR FRITH WOOD

Route 11

Woodland Walk Near Ledbury

Outline   Knapp Lane ~ Frith Wood ~ Wellington Heath ~ Beggar's Ash ~ Doghill Wood (optional) ~ Knapp Lane.

Summary   Despite the fact that throughout its entire distance, this walk is never more than a couple of miles from the little town of Ledbury, this in no way spoils the heart-of-the-country feeling that prevails right from the start. Woodland is the principal attraction, but variety in the form of field paths, a village street and a large fruit farm enrich the route, as do the views of the surrounding countryside on the return stage of the walk.

Attractions   Frith Wood is an extensive tract of mixed woodland, owned and maintained by the Forestry Commission. The woodland walk is along a so-called permissive path, as distinct from a right-of-way.

   The trees, wild flowers, birds and insects inhabiting large woods like this are so many and varied that there is plenty to see at all times of the year. The large mature trees are chiefly oak, birch, sweet chestnut and wild cherry (bearer of beautiful blossom). There are also some ancient yew alongside the track and a very old lime tree on the left at the brow of the slope, which is well worth a closer look. A good deal of the wood is given over to hazel, the nut-bearing shrub often found along hedgerows. Notice that the hazels have been coppiced, that is they have been cut off just above ground level, and new wood has grown from the severed stumps. Coppicing is an ancient woodland craft, carried out at regular intervals (between seven and fifteen years) to produce timber for fencing, charcoal and firewood.

   Woodland flowers are usually at their best early in spring, before the canopy of leaves closes over the woodland floor, shutting out the light. During April and May, the fringe of the wood bordering the path is a riot of colour. Watch out especially for bluebell (impossible to miss!), the delicate white wood anemone and the smaller wood sorrel.

   Frith Wood has a varied bird population. Among the largest and noisest residents is the jay, a gaudily-coloured member of the crow family, which makes off with a harsh squawking cry at our approach. Another noisy bird is the green woodpecker, whose laughing call echoes through the trees for a great distance. Smaller birds include several species of tit and from April onwards, three small olive-grey warblers especially noted for their distinctive songs - the chiffchaff, the willow warbler and the blackcap.

continued on page 52

49

Route 11

Route 11

Woodland Walk Near Ledbury 4½ miles

START   *Layby at the summit of Knapp Lane, Ledbury. Reached from the A449 (Malvern road) by taking a minor road signposted 'Coddington 4'. The layby is at a road junction soon after the crossroads.* (O.S. Sheet 149. GR 715386).

ROUTE

1. *To avoid the busy, dangerous road, pass through a gap in the fence at the extremity of the layby and in 20 metres turn through a hedge on the right and follow the descending path parallel to the road. Where the path meets the road, cross with great care and in a short distance, turn right at a 'Public footpath' sign along a metalled road. Pass Tunnel Cottage which stands directly over the tunnel which takes the Ledbury-to-Malvern railway line through Bradlow Knoll.*

2. *At the entrance to the drive to Frith Wood House, ignore a stile on the left (return route). Instead, keep straight on along the drive past the house. The drive now becomes a forest road. Follow this road for about 1½ miles, ignoring all side turnings, however tempting. Eventually, at a junction, keep left, to arrive shortly at a small car park. At the end of the park, turn sharp left under a holly tree.*

3. *The footpath keeps the wood on the left for about 400 metres until the field on the right ends. Here, cross a stile on the right into a field. Keeping a hedgerow on the right, go through a gate, ignoring a footpath through another gate on the right. Keep straight on to the bottom of the field. Cross two stiles and a footbridge into a field. Turn left and follow the stream through a gateway into the next field. In about 50 metres, turn right to cross this field, aiming slightly to the left of a telephone pole, beyond which a stile leads to Wellington Heath (and Farmers Arms Inn).*

4. *The route continues along the road to the left of the inn. At a right bend, turn left and cross a stile by Long Acre. Cross the sloping field downhill to a stile. Cross the brook and climb half-right between fruit trees to some large sheds at Beggar's Ash.*

5. *Turn left towards a house and at a drive entrance climb between fruit trees on the right to a cottage (Little Frith). Pass through the garden and along a fence bordering Frith Wood House to the stile passed earlier.*

51

*Back at the road, either return direct to the car **or** cross the road and climb the steps into Doghill wood. Follow the path behind the houses to a crossroads of paths with a bench nearby. Turn left to skirt the woodland back to the car.*

By contrast, activities on the fruit farm are worth noting throughout the changing year. Weed and pest control, pruning and most interesting of all - harvesting - may rekindle the young walker's flagging interest on the concluding stages of the walk.

Refreshments The Farmers Arms, Wellington Heath. Bar meals. Terrace. Children welcome.

Extra attraction Ledbury is a delightful little market town with plenty to see. The Old Market House dates back to 1633. Church Lane is a narrow cobbled thoroughfare full of interest. Notice too, the distinctive clock tower and almshouses.

LOWER BROCKHAMPTON

52

Route 12   2½ miles

(Optional 2¾ miles extra to Lower Brockhampton)

Bromyard Downs

Outline   Brockhampton school ~ Warren Wood ~ Shepherd Cottage ~ Warren Farm ~ Lower Brockhampton Diversion ~ Brockhampton school.

Summary   Open downland is a rare feature of the Herefordshire countryside, most of such common land having been enclosed during the last century or earlier. The quaint little town of Bromyard is fortunate in having a sizeable tract of this land still intact however, and this walk includes part of it, as well as woodland, with a lengthy diversion to see the National Trust property of Lower Brockhampton as an optional extension to what is otherwise a short, easy walk.

Attractions   The sheep-nibbled turf interspersed with clumps of bracken make an ideal place for children's play on this hillside east of Bromyard. Grown-ups may well prefer to spend the time admiring the open views. Nearby Warren Wood consists of an interesting mixture of timber, including oak, beech, sycamore, birch, yew and Scots pine.

The garden of Shepherd Cottage is sure to appeal to children. It is full of intriguing models, depicting buildings, animals and other assorted representations, the most striking of which is a painstakingly-accurate model of Lower Brockhampton manor house. This may well persuade reluctant young walkers that the somewhat lengthy diversion later on is worth the effort.

The diversion itself provides a change of scenery as well as a few surprises. The first of these is a charming Gothic revival church which was built in 1798 and although kept locked, adds a romantic touch to the walk as it rises above the trees. Just beyond, in the wall bordering the grounds of the private red-brick mansion of Brockhampton Park, is a door leading to an ice house, a necessary feature in a country house in the days before refrigeration. Blocks of ice were hauled up to this building from the nearby lake.

The tree-lined approach to Lower Brockhampton offers the chance to study woodland bird life. In spring, thrushes, finches, tits and warblers can be heard in full song and woodpeckers add variety with their laughter and drumming.

It is something of an understatement to say that Lower Brockhampton lives up to its enviable reputation. The exquisite group of

continued on page 56

53

Route 12

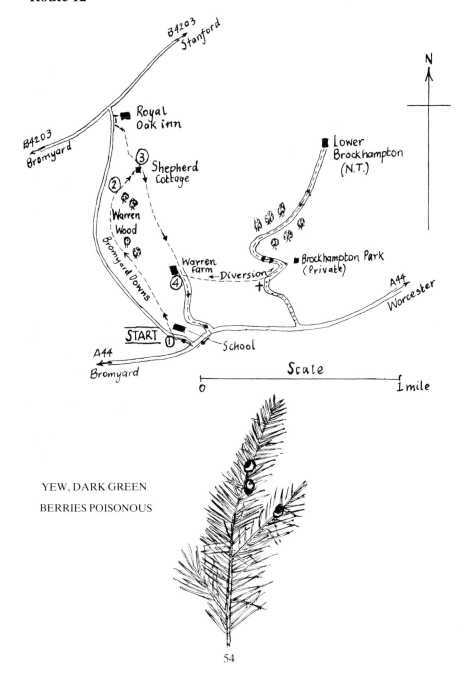

YEW, DARK GREEN

BERRIES POISONOUS

54

Route 12

Bromyard Downs

2½ miles

(Optional 2 miles extra to Lower Brockhampton)

START *At a lay-by opposite Brockhampton Primary Schook, on minor road signposted 'Bromyard Downs', just off the A44, 1½ miles east of Bromyard. (O.S. Sheet 149 GR 678543) Park in lay-by.*

ROUTE

1. *From the lay-by, cross the minor road and reach the Downs through the gap to the left of the school. Climb the slope and, when the track begins to dip, enter Warren Wood through a handgate on the right. Follow the path that keeps to the left-hand edge of the wood. Eventually, this well-worn path veers to the right and climbs to the woodland limit.*

2. *Leave the wood by a stile on the left. Keep straight on along the edge of a field with a narrow wood to the right to arrive at the gate to Shepherd Cottage. (Those wishing to visit the Royal Oak Inn should descend the track on the left and then turn right for a short distance along the minor road. Retrace your steps to the cottage.)*

3. *To resume the walk from Shepherd Cottage, follow the footpath to the left of the cottage to a kissing-gate. Pass through the gate and follow a footpath with a hedge on the left. Go through a gate by a pond and straight on, with a hedge' now on the right, to join a lane leading to Warren Farm.*

   Diversion *The diversion to Lower Brockhampton (2¾ miles and involving the retracing of steps) begins at Warren Farm. To include it, turn left just before the cattle grid near the farm and follow the straight track, which gives access to parkland through a gate. Keep on along the grassy track, which is joined by a metalled drive coming in on the right by a chapel. Keep on along the drive, following its winding course through parkland and woods down to Lower Brockhampton.*

4. *To continue the walk, cross the cattle grid and follow the farm drive to its junction with the A44. Turn right (the opposite verge is safer to walk on) and proceed the short distance to the minor road to Bromyard Downs from which the walk began.*

ACCESS BY BUS

Bromyard is connected by bus with Hereford and Worcester. (Midland Red West)

55

medieval buildings stand at the end of the long approach lane, breathtaking almost in their timeless beauty. We are told that the little half-timbered gatehouse is about a hundred years more recent than the hall itself but with such a time-scale this matters little. Entering the main building we see how the basic cruck design was skilfully adapted to support a much larger-than-normal building, and how the craftsmen of old combined grace and strength to create a gem of 14th century architecture.

Nearby attraction   The little town of Bromyard is well worth wandering around. Its status has declined over the years, which may have something to do with its appeal. Many of the fine black-and-white houses date from the 17th century, although the grammar school (now part of the primary school) was established as long ago as 1394.

Refreshments   The Royal Oak, Norton Downs, Bromyard. Snacks and lunches. Enclosed gardens. Children's play area.

EARDISLAND

The Arrow Valley
Pembridge to Eardisland

Outline   Pembridge ~ fieldpath by River Arrow ~ Eardisland ~ Pembridge.

Summary   Pembridge and Eardisland are both tourist attractions and as such, feature on the itineraries of many motorists, especially during the summer months. This walk is intended to enable families to enjoy both villages - and the delightful scenery in which they lie - on foot, yet at the same time avoiding most of the traffic that can make walking a hazardous occupation. The river-walk section of the route can be wet in places after rain and strong footwear is advised.

Attractions   Pembridge was a market town during the Middle Ages and as many of its most appealing buildings are survivors from that time, a leisurely walkabout is strongly recommended. A good place to begin exploring is the market hall, built in the early 16th century with carved oak pillars supporting a stone tiled roof. Timber is the most prominent building material to catch the eye in Pembridge, which boasts a higher number of houses of cruck construction than anywhere else in Herefordshire. From the market hall a flight of stone steps leads up to the church, which has a detached bell-tower similar in shape to a pagoda.

Eardisland, by contrast, is a small village which has made the most of its idyllic situation on the banks of the Arrow. Perhaps the most appealing of its houses, Staick House, is said to date from the 14th century but children will be more interested in the old timber-framed school with its whipping-post nearby.

The riverside walk linking the two villages is a nature-lover's paradise throughout spring and early summer. The low-lying meadows echo with the plaintive bubbling calls of curlews - long legged, curved-beaked birds that return here from distant river estuaries to breed each year. Mallard also find the damp conditions to their liking, while dragonflies of several different species haunt the river bank. For centuries, the River Arrow was known as a favoured haunt of that fine native mammal, the otter. Sadly, its increasing rarity means that a sighting is now extremely unlikely, but it is always worth keeping a sharp lookout.

Although it is used by a little local traffic, the winding lane back to Pembridge makes a pleasant contrast after the fieldpath by the river.

continued on page 60

Route 13

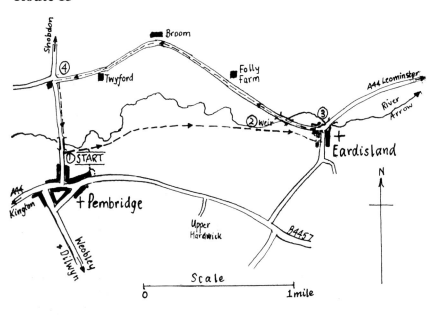

ALDER,

FRUIT BROWN, CATKINS

Feb.-March

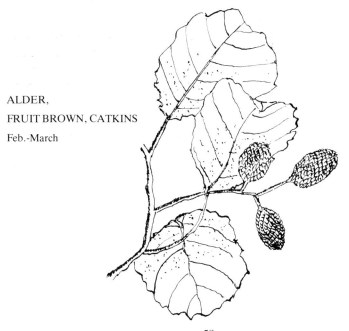

58

Route 13

The Arrow Valley

5 miles

Pembridge to Eardisland

START   *Pembridge village, on the A44 midway between Leominster and Kington* (O.S. Sheets 148 or 149. GR 390580). *Park in village.*

ROUTE

1. *From the A44, follow the minor Shobdon-Presteigne road north down to the bridge over the River Arrow. Just before the bridge, turn right along the bank-side track. In a short distance, leave the river and cross a stile by the right hand of 2 gates. Pass a sewage farm and enter a field on the left. Keep a hedge and a brook on the right, following the hedge round to the left at the extremity of the field, to pass through a gate and into another field. Beyond the gate, bear right along the hedge to continue along the line walked previously. Keep the hedge on the right through the next field and pass into another field through a gate. Cross a plank bridge on the left and keep on half-left towards the river, aiming for 2 large oaks in the middle of the field. Beyond the trees, veer left to cross a stile close to the river. Beyond cleared woodland, bear right to pass through a gate and keep left, with a fence and an avenue of poplars on the left, to arrive at a stile by the river with a weir to the left.*

2. *Cross the stile and bear right to follow the left hand edge of an oak wood. Beyond the wood, keep a hedge on the right round a field. When the field narrows, cross a double stile on the right. Turn left along the hedge (Eardisland church is visible ahead) to cross a triple stile on the left. Bear right across a field and go through a hedge-gap to reach Eardisland.*

3. *Leave Eardisland along a lane signposted 'Unsuitable for long vehicles'. Follow the lane on its winding course, passing Folly, Broom and Twyford farms to reach a T-junction.*

4. *Turn left to cross the Arrow at the starting point of the walk and climb the slope back to Pembridge.*

Some of the hedges bordering the lane are very old and consequently rich in the number of species of trees and shrubs they contain. Watch out for hawthorn, blackthorn, hazel, field maple, holly, dogwood, ash and wild cherry, as well as alder trees in the vicinity of the river.

Plane-spotters will no doubt notice the activity going on at Shobdon airfield, a few miles north, where parachute-jumping often takes place. Railway enthusiasts will recognise the house opposite the junction of the lane with the road back to Pembridge near the end of the walk as the converted railway station, from which trains could once be caught to Kington and Leominster.

Refreshments These are obtainable both in Pembridge and Eardisland.

LUGG BRIDGE, MARDEN

Lugg Valley and Sutton Walls

Outline   Moreton Bridge ~ Sutton St. Michael ~ Sutton Walls ~ Marden village ~ Marden Church ~ Moreton Bridge.

Summary   From its source on the edge of Radnor Forest, the River Lugg flows in a south-easterly direction to meet the Wye close by Hereford at Mordiford. The grassy footpaths in the lower Lugg Valley make for pleasant walking, as families following this route will discover. Children will relish hearing some of the stories - both fact and fantasy - that have their origins in this corner of Herefordshire, and these, together with plenty of wild-life interest, combine to ensure that this walk, if not spectacular, has something for all the family.

Attractions   For much of its length, the Lugg is a secret river, gliding almost furtively beneath ancient stone bridges, two of which can be seen on this walk. But it is the stretch of river-bank walking between Marden's Bridge and its lonely church that offers the closest acquaintance with the river, and children will savour the experience all the more when told the tale of the mermaid and the bell.

The story goes that in the 13th century, when workmen were hanging a bell in the old church steeple, it fell into the river, where it was claimed by a mermaid, who refused to return it. The men decided to wait until the mermaid was asleep and then to snatch it back. When at last the mermaid fell asleep, the men set out in a boat to recover the bell. As they approached their objective however, one of them called out 'Steady' and this woke the mermaid, who, together with the bell, was carried upstream in a violent storm, which caused the pursuing boat to capsize. Eventually, both bell and mermaid sank from view in deep water and were never seen again, although it is said that occasionally, when the bells of nearby churches ring out, an echoing toll can be heard from beneath the waters of the River Lugg!

Strange tales too, are told about Sutton Walls, the vast Iron-Age fort perched on a hilltop not far away. Excavations have revealed that it was occupied until late Roman times and that its 30-acre site held many timber-framed buildings. Some people believe that the Saxon King Offa, the Dyke builder, had a castle on the hilltop over 1,000 years ago and that it was here that Ethelbert, King of East Anglia, who was visiting Offa to seek the hand of his daughter in marriage, was brutally murdered. According to legend, the dead king was first buried in Marden Church,

continued on page 64

Route 14

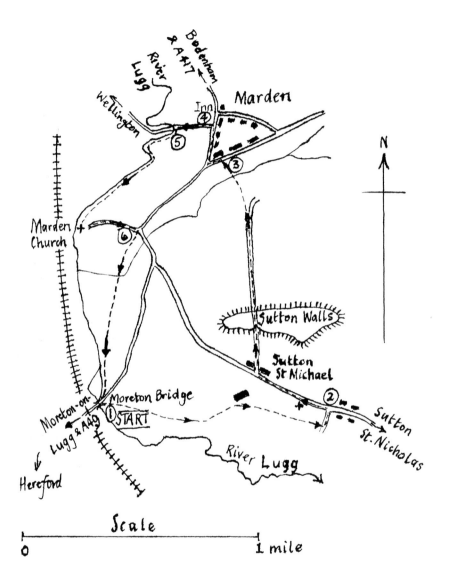

Route 14

Lugg Valley & Sutton Walls
4½ miles

START   *Moreton Bridge, ½ mile east of Moreton-on-Lugg. Leave the A49 (Hereford to Leominster) road at signpost 'Village Centre ¼, Marden 2'. Limited parking near the bridge. (O.S. Sheet 149. GR 513459).*

ROUTE

1. *From the direction of Moreton, cross the bridge and climb the stile on the right alongside the gate with a 'Private Fishing' sign. Strike out across the field with a barbedwire fence on the left. Where the fence ends, pass through a gap and go straight on across another field with spaced-out hawthorn bushes now on the left. After climbing another stile, veer slightly to the left across the next field and, after crossing a fenced ditch over a cart bridge, keep the ditch on the right and soon climb a fence at the corner of a small wood. Keep the wood-side on the left as far as a farm (Freens Court). Go through a gate to the right of the farm wall and cross a large field, keeping on a straight course roughly parallel to, and 150 metres distant from, the road-hedge on the left. Cross a stile (possibly overgrown) and keep straight on under power lines to a stile alongside a metal gate. (A chapel can be seen on the left). In the next field, make for a metal gate at the top left-hand corner to reach a lane. Turn left to join a road. (Note: growing crops can make walking difficult from Freens Court onwards and it may be easier to walk round the edge of one or more fields).*

2. *From the junction, turn left (ignoring a bridle path opposite). After a right-hand bend, turn right along a metalled road between two houses. Climb over a locked gate and ascend the slope, with Sutton Walls ahead. At the top of the slope, where the metalled path veers right, keep straight on through a gateway to enter a small wood. From the wood, keep on into the first of 2 fields with an orchard on the right beyond the hedge. In the third and fourth fields, the hedge is on the left. Midway down the fourth field, cross a stile in the hedge and keep alongside the fence. Go through a gate and keep straight on between bungalows to reach a road.*

3. *Turn left and then right at a junction. At the next junction, signposted Wellington to the left, the Volunteer Inn can be seen straight ahead.*

4. *Follow the Wellington road as far as the River Lugg. Just before the bridge, turn left over a stile.*

5. *Follow the river along its left bank. Marden Church soon appears ahead. Cross a stile under the willows to the right of a house (the*

vicarage) and another by the river bank to enter the churchyard. Leave the churchyard by the main drive, crossing a cattle grid with the vicarage on the left. At the end of the lane, watch out for a stile on the right beneath a pine tree.

6. *Cross the stile into a field and continue parallel with a stream on the left, as far as a bridge between 2 willow trees. The path leads straight across the next field, through a gate and over another field to a stile, with the river a short distance to the right. The stile to the road near Moreton Bridge is about 50 metres from the river bank.*

---

but was late re-buried in Hereford Cathedral by the contrite Offa, and a healing spring then flowed from the little church on the bank of the Lugg.

The wild life of the lower Lugg Valley is an added bonus on this walk. The crowns of ancient willows overhanging the river contain a range of opportunist wind-blown and bird-carried plants. Watch out too, for dainty grey wagtails flitting along above the water. Fishermen claim that the Lugg is one of the best rivers in the country for grayling.

Refreshments The Volunteer Inn, Marden. Snacks, bar meals, morning coffee. Children welcome.

MORDIFORD BRIDGE

64

Route 15

Fownhope to Mordiford

Outline   Fownhope ~ Fiddler's Green ~ West Wood ~ Mordiford ~ Bagpiper's Tump ~ Hope Springs ~ Fownhope.

Summary   This walk, the only one in the book routed along the Wye Valley (which is the subject of another book in the Family Walks series) - combines woodland and open-country walking through delightful scenery. Add to that plenty of scope for wildlife -watching and a look at two villages, each rich in historical associations and the result is a memorable day-out for all the family.

Attractions   Few would challenge the claim, made in a recent book about the Wye, that it is the loveliest and most unspoilt of our largest rivers. At Fownhope, despite having left Hereford and the Welsh hills far behind, the Wye still retains much of its magic, as this walk shows.

Fownhope is a large village by Herefordshire standards, with plenty to see. It is said that there are no less than 22,000 oak shingles on the broached spire of the parish church, which contains a beautiful Norman tympanum over a doorway, depicting the Virgin Mary holding the baby Jesus. The 9-foot long parish chest is over 500 years old and was made from a single piece of oak. Near the church can be seen stocks and a whipping post, while not far away is a milestone informing the curious that Hereford is exactly 6¼ miles and 56 yards distant.

There is an extensive children's playground near the start of the walk, which serves as a useful incentive to young walkers to 'complete the course'.

The woodland walk to Mordiford teems with interest for the young naturalist. The presence of so many yew trees near the prehistoric fort indicates that this is ancient woodland, a view supported by the rich ground flora, in which dog's mercury is abundant. Both deer and badgers inhabit these woods. Deer prints are easy to spot on muddy turf, while badger dung-pits can be seen under low vegetation. Bird life includes jays, woodpeckers, tits and goldcrests.

Mordiford is best known for its ancient bridge, which spans the River Lugg just before its confluence with the Wye. The main western arch dates from 1352. In bygone times, the lord of the manor of Mordiford had to present the king with a pair of gilt spurs every time he crossed the bridge, but there is no record of the eventual size of the Royal-spur-collection!

continued on page 68

Route 15

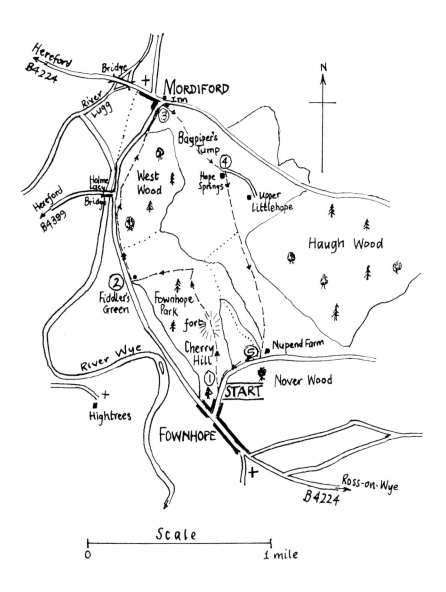

Route 15

Fownhope to Mordiford   4½ miles

START *Fownhope village, on the B4224 between Hereford and Ross-on-Wye* (O.S. Sheet No. 149, GR 580343). *Park in the village.*

ROUTE

1. *Take the road signposted 'Woolhope 3'. Just beyond the last house on the left, watch for a footpath sign on the left. Climb the steps into a wood. In a short distance, take the right-hand path at a fork and keep straight on, ignoring side tracks. The winding path climbs through the trees to the remains of a hill-fort and then dips to another fork. Bear right down the steps under the yew trees. At a junction of paths, turn left and at the next, right, to climb to the top of a slope, where the conifers end. From here, follow a narrow path on the left, which dips steeply through the bracken to meet a track coming in from the right. Keep straight on down the track, passing some houses to reach a road.*

2. *This is Fiddler's Green. Turn right along the road. Just beyond Wyedown House, take the signposted path on the right, which passes beneath the trees to a stile by a gate. Follow the clear path through the woods to emerge on the road once more at the approach to Mordiford. The Moon Inn lies straight ahead.*

3. *The return route commences in the mill yard, and begins along the course of the Wye Valley Walk, marked by yellow arrows. Cross two cart bridges and ascend a slope between a hedge (on the right) and an orchard (on the left) to reach a lane over a stile. Bear left (Bagpiper's Tump) to reach a farm (Hope Springs).*

4. *Turn right between the farm buildings and follow the straight track ahead. Opposite some cottages, ignore a track on the right and keep straight on in a field with a hedge on the left. Continue straight on to reach a road.*

5. *Turn right back to Fownhope, passing the start of the walk on the way.*

No young walker should leave Mordiford without hearing the story of its famous dragon. It is a long time since its picture could be seen on the church wall - a visit to Hereford museum is necessary to see what it looked like - but the story lives on. Apparently the dragon, then quite small, was found by a girl called Maud, who despite her father's opposition, insisted in rearing it until it became too big to handle. The dragon then began killing and eating other animals - and people, too - until one day a condemned criminal agred to kill it in return for his freedom. He hid with his bow and arrow in a cider barrel and shot the beast through the bung-hole, but as the creature died, its fiery breath set fire to the barrel and the luckless prisoner died, too.

Refreshments The Moon Inn, Mordiford. Snacks and lunches. Garden. Children welcome.

THE GREAT OAK, EARDISLEY

Route 16

Almeley and Eardisley

Walk 1 - Almeley

Outline   Almeley ~ Nieuport House ~ Almeley Wotton ~ Almeley.

Summary   This is a pleasant, easy country walk along fieldpaths and minor roads, concluding with a delightful stretch of footpath along a brook known locally as the Batch. The local history is interesting and wildlife varied.

Attractions   Although castle remains are common in Welsh border country, Almeley is remarkable in having had two, both of which are passed on this walk. The first lies in a field to the south of the church and is believed to have been built in the 13th century. All that can be seen now is the mound, known as a motte, with signs of the bailey, or enclosed area, to the north. A dry ditch, once a moat, surrounds the remains. Not far away to the south are two hollows which were fishponds, dug to supply the castle with a handy source of food.

Border castles are often known as twts, from the Saxon word toot, or lookout place. The second castle mound passed along the Batch brook, is known as Oldcastle twt, and was the home of Sir John Oldcastle, a 14th century nobleman on whom Shakespeare is said to have based his character Sir John Falstaff.

The bird, insect and botanical life along the Batch brook is well worth noting. Robins, wrens, tits and chaffinches are joined in spring by warblers. Watch for speckled wood butterflies in the dappled light. Flowers include sanicle, betony and burdock. Ferns such as polypody and male fern thrive in the damp shade.

Walk 2 - Eardisley

Outline   The church ~ the castle mound ~ the bridleway ~ the fieldpath ~ the great oak ~ the street ~ the church.

Summary   This short walk is essentially a village walkabout, of the kind that can be taken around almost any village, in Herefordshire or elsewhere. Eardisley, however, is a somewhat special village, as can be seen from what follows.

Attractions   No visitor to Eardisley, however young, should miss seeing the 12th-century font in the church, with its carvings of fighting knights and a fascinating representation of a lion. The castle, on a mound veiled

continued on page 72

69

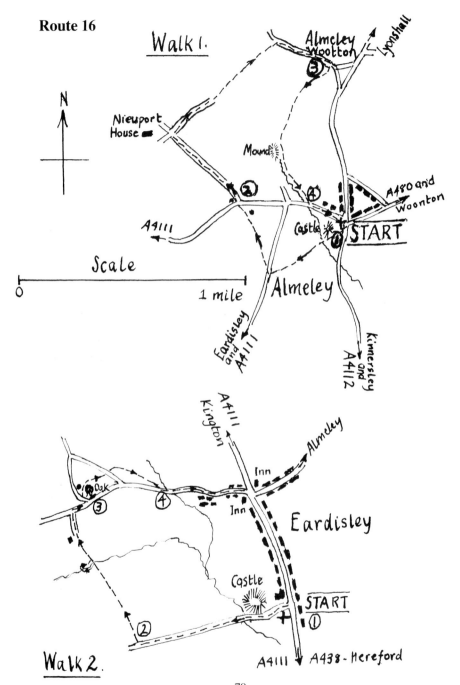

Walk 1.

N

Walk 2.

Route 16

Almeley & Eardisley   2 walks, each of 3 miles

Walk 1

START   *Almeley Church. Almeley lies within the Kington-Eardisley-Weobley triangle, roughly midway between the A4111, A4112 and A480. (O.S. Sheet 148, GR 333515). Park as near as possible to the church.*

ROUTE

1. *Just south of the church, along the Kinnersley road, climb a stile at a 'Public Footpath' sign on the right. Pass the castle mound and ditch on the right, followed by the remains of the fishponds, and dip down to a stile and a bridge. Cross the bridge and continue in the same direction to an orchard. Go through in the same direction and over a stile into a wood. Cross a narrow field to reach a road. Cross and climb the stile alongside a gate. The path lies half-right across the next field, so aim for the gate about 50 yards to the left of a large oak tree near the fence. Go through the gate and aim for another ahead in front of some farm buildings. Now keep the fence on the left, cross 2 stiles and reach a road by a lodge and postbox.*

2. *Cross the road and walk along the drive towards Nieuport House. At a crossroads of paths almost level with the house, turn right. Pass a walled garden then a house on the right and a farm on the left, and cross a stile by a gate straight ahead. Keep a hedge on the right over a field, go through a gate, cross a track and go straight over another field, aiming for the far left-hand corner. Go through the right of 2 gates and keep a hedge on the left. A red-roofed house can now be seen ahead. At the end of the field, climb a shallow bank to reach a road by the house. Turn right along the road for Almeley Wootton.*

3. *At the entrance to the village, where a stony track dips into woodland on the right by some black and white posts, follow it, passing some cottages along the stream bank. Eventually, at the foot of the slope up to the second castle mound, take the left-hand path along the stream to cross 2 bridges and reach a gravelled lane by a house. Follow this lane to reach a road.*

4. *Turn left. Almeley Church soon comes into view on the right.*

Walk 2

START   *Eardisley Church. Eardisley is two miles south-west of Almeley and stands on the A4111, six miles south of Kington. Park by the church.* (O.S. Sheet 148, GR 312492).

ROUTE

1. *Follow the lane alongside the church. It soon becomes a bridleway, passing the castle remains on the right. In about a mile, as the bridleway bends to the right to approach Eardisley Park Farm, watch for a stile in the hedge on the right.*
2. *Cross the stile and keep hedges on the right through 3 fields. Cross a stream (the footbridge may be missing - if so, follow the hedge to the left to cross by a cartbridge and retrace the route back to the original line). Keep straight on to meet a drive by a house. Climb up to the road and turn right. The Eardisley Oak is on the left along the lane by a chapel.*
3. *From the Oak, follow a signposted footpath through a cemetery and over a stile. Keep a hedge on the left and reach a road through a gate. Turn left, and in 20 metres, right over a stile. Keep to the right, following a stream until the narrowing field meets a road at a gate.*
4. *Go through the gate and turn left along the road to Eardisley. The church is along the street to the right.*

―――――――――

by trees and on private land, was destroyed during the Civil War after an eventful history.

A local historian has produced a map of the field names of the village as they appeared in 1841. Those fields on the left of the fieldpath were known as White Gate Field, Lower Tynings, Lowbitch Meadow, Lower Lawn and Piece by the Common, while those to the right of the route were named 14 Acres, Bear Croft, Upper Rems, Field by the Yapp and New Lands. Children may enjoy speculating on the origins of some of these names.

The Great Oak is one of England's veteran trees. There is room inside for the largest family. Notice how it has been damaged by fire, yet still survives.

The Tram Inn got its name from a horse-tramway, which connected the village with Kington. There was a railway here too, until the Second World War. Nearby is a fine cruck cottage. The walk along the village street reveals many interesting buildings, including a row of cottages converted from a timber-framed barn with a cider-press in the garden.

Refreshments New Inn, Eardisley. Morning coffee. Bar meals. Children's play area.

Appendices

HERGEST RIDGE   - over the hill to Wales -   4¼ miles

Summary   This one-way hill walk, from Kington to Gladestry, is included as an optional extra for those families in which a driver is willing to forego participating in the walk or is prepared to set out to meet up with the party after having parked the car at the destination.

Attractions   Keen young walkers will enjoy the challenge and achievement of climbing from Kington to the 1,375-foot summit of Hergest Ridge by the Offa's Dyke Path and descending to cross into Wales at the village of Gladestry. The route passes Hergest Croft Gardens (which are open to the public and are famous for their collections of rhododendrons, maples and birches) and climbs to the site of an old racecourse. Nearby is the Whet Stone, which according to legend derived its name from wheat, brought here for the people of Kington to collect during the Black Death in the 14th century, to avoid the plague from spreading. However, a more fanciful myth relates that the stone has a wandering habit and goes down to drink at the stream below the ridge when it hears the morning cock crow!

This stretch of the Offa's Dyke long distance footpath is clearly indicated by marker posts but the wild terrain and sweeping views create an atmosphere of remoteness which cannot fail to appeal to children's sense of adventure. From the path, once an old drovers' road, can be seen rain-filled pools, which are made use of by the sheep and ponies on the Ridge. The boulders scattered around were deposited by the melting ice-sheet over 10,000 years ago.

Bird life on the Ridge is limited to buzzards, kestrels, skylarks and meadow pipits. As the path drops down towards Gladestry, it is worth watching out for tits, nuthatches and pied flycatchers - all of which can be seen along the wooded approach to the village during the summer months.

Both swifts and house martins nest in good numbers in Gladestry. The swifts make use of the eaves of the chancel of St. Mary's church while the house martins prefer those of the farmhouse bearing the 1689 datestone nearby.

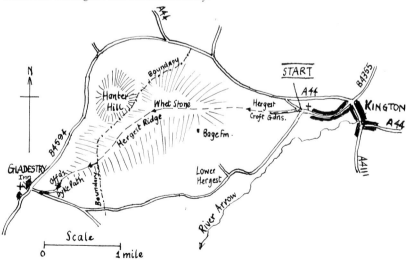

HERGEST RIDGE

4¼ miles

- over the hill to Wales -

START   *Kington. From the centre of the town, drive in a north-westerly direction, climbing past the church on the right. After passing the minor road to Gladestry on the left, watch out for another left turning just over the brow of the hill, signposted 'Ridgebourne and Hergest Croft.' The walk begins here. (O.S. Sheet 148, GR 290567).*

ROUTE - for driver.

Proceed to Gladestry either along minor road or via the A44 and B4594 to meet the walking party, either at the Royal Oak Inn or along the route. If walking to meet the party from the Royal Oak, turn right and right again before taking the Offa's Dyke Path about 100 metres on the left. Climb the path, passing through two gates and out on to open country.

ROUTE - for walkers.

From the starting point, keep straight on along the signposted lane, passing Hergest Croft Gardens. Ignore all side turns. The lane eventually becomes a rough track. Pass through a gate and continue climbing over the sheep-nibbled turf, following the marker posts with their acorn symbols. Beyond the old racecourse and the Whet Stone, the path soon begins its gradual descent, leaving Hanter Hill away to the right and eventually descending to pass through two gates and so along the wide path to Gladestry. At the foot of the path, turn right then left to reach the Royal Oak Inn.

ROUTES IN ORDER OF DIFFICULTY

Easy short walks *(less than 5 miles)*

Route   7 - *Salwarpe and Droitwitch Canal*
Route 11 - *Woodland walk near Ledbury*
Route 12 - *Bromyard Downs (Excluding Lower Brockhampton)*
Route 16 - Almeley only
Route 16 - *Eardisley only.*

More strenuous walks *(less than 5 miles)*

Route   1 - *A Cotswold Corner*
Route   8 - *Abberley Hill*
Route   9 - *The Malvern Hills - North*
Route 14 - *Lugg Valley and Sutton Walls*
Route 15 - *Fownhope to Mordiford*
One-way walk   *Hergest Ridge.*

Easy longer walks *(5 or more miles)*

Route   3 - *Avon valley and Cleeve Prior*
Route   4 - *Pershore and Tyddesley Wood*
Route   5 - *The Worcester and Birmingham Canal*
Route   6 - *Wyre Forest*
Route 12 - *Bromyard Downs (Including Lower Brockhampton)*
Route 13 - *Pembridge to Erdisland*
Route 16 - *Almeley and Eardisley (both walks)*

More strenuous longer walk *(5 or more miles)*

Route   2 - *Bredon Hill.*

WET WEATHER ALTERNATIVES - completely or partly under cover.

MUSEUMS AND ART GALLERIES

Almonry Museum, Abbey Gate, Evesham. Open Easter-September.

Avoncroft Museum of Buildings, Stoke Heath, near Bromsgrove. Open March-November.

Bewdley Museum, The Shambles, Load Street. Open March-November.

Bromsgrove Museum, 26 Birmingham Road, Bromsgrove (also Craft Centre). Open all year.

Churchill Gardens Museum, Venns Lane, Hereford.

City Museum and Art Gallery, Foregate St. Worcester. Open all year.

City Museum and Art Gallery, Broad Street, Hereford. Open all year.

Coningsby Chapel and Museum, Widemarsh Street, Hereford. Open Easter-September.

Droitwich Heritage Centre, Heritage Way, Droitwich. Open all year.

Hereford Cider Museum, Pomona Place, Whitecross Road Hereford. Open April-October.

Herefordshire Light Infantry Regimental Museum, Harold Street, Hereford. By appointment only.

Herefordshire Rural Heritage Museum, Doward, Symonds Yat, Ross-on-Wye. Open all year.

Herefordshire Waterworks Museum, Broom Hill, Hereford. Open June-September.

Leominster Folk Museum, Etnam Street. Open March-November.

The Commandery, Civil War Centre, Sidbury, Worcester. Open all year.

The Old House, High Town, Hereford. Limited opening throughout year.

The Tudor House Museum, Friar Street, Worcester. Open all year.

Worcestershire County Museum, Hartlebury Castle, near Kidderminster. Open March-November.

HISTORIC BUILDINGS - open to the public.

Berrington Hall, near Leominster (NT) Open May-September.

Bredon Tithe Barn (NT) Open Daily.

Bordesley Abbey, Redditch (Ruins - open all year).

Burton Court, near Eardisland. Open May-September.

Croft Castle, near Leominster (NT) Open May-September.

Dinmore Manor, Westhope, near Leominster. Open all year.

Eastmor Castle, near Ledbury. Limited opening during Summer months.

Goodrich Castle, near Ross-on-Wye (English Heritage) Open all year.

Greyfriars, Friar Street, Worcester (NT) Limited opening April-October.

Guildhall, Worcester. Open all year - Monday-Friday.

Hanbury Hall, near Droitwich. (NT). Open April-October.

Harvington Hall, near Kidderminster. Open April-November.

Hawford Dovecote, 3 miles noth of Worcester off A449 (NT).

Lower Brockhampton, nr Bromyard (NT) Limited opening March-October.

Middle Littleton Tithe Barn, 3 miles N.E. of Evesham (NT).

Moccas Court, near Bredwardine. Open April-September.

Wichenford Dovecote, 5½ miles N.W. of Worcester off B4204 (NT).

OTHER PLACES OF INTEREST - completely or partly under cover.

ARTS AND CRAFT CENTRES

Annard Woollen Mill, Handgate Farm, Church Lench, near Evesham.

The Jinney Ring Craft Centre, Hanbury, near Bromsgrove. Open Easter-Christmas. Limited opening.

INDUSTRIAL INTEREST.

Bulmer Railway Centre, Whitecross Road, Hereford. Open Easter-September (Weekends).

Forge Mill National Needle Museum, Needle Mill Lane, Redditch. Open all year.

Midland Bus and Transport Musuem, Chapel Lane, Wythall. Open weekends and Bank Holidays. April-November.

Severn Valley Railway, Railway Station, Bewdley.

Worcester Royal Porcelain and Dyson Perrins Museum. Open all year.

WILD LIFE.

Birchfield Waterfowl, Upper Rochford, Tenbury Wells. Open weekends Easter-October.

Symonds Yat Bird Park, Symonds Yat West, near Ross-on-Wye. Open all year.

The Domestic Fowl Trust, Honeybourne, near Evesham. Open all year.

The World of Butterflies, Whitchurch, near Ross-on-Wye. Open daily April-October.

West Midland Safari and Leisure Park, Spring Grove, Bewdley.

Wyre Forest Visitors Centre, near Bewdley. Open all year.

OTHER PARKS, GARDENS, TRAILS AND VIEWPOINTS.

Broadway Tower Country Park, Open April-October.

Burford House Gardens, near Tenbury Wells. Open March-November.

Clacks Farm, Boreley, Ombersley, Worcester. Open selected weekends. Spring-Autumn.

Clent Hills Country Park, near Birmingham.

Hartlebury Common, near Stourport-on-Severn.

Hergest Croft Gardens, near Kington. Open April-October.

Queenswood Country Park, (between Hereford and Leominster).

Spetchley Park, near Worcester. Open April-September.

The Jubilee Maze, Symonds Yat, Ross-on-Wye. Open daily April-October.

The Weir, (5 miles West of Hereford on A438) (NT). Open March-October.

Twyford Country Centre, Evesham. Open all year.

Waseley Hills Country Park, near Bromsgrove.

Worcester Woods Country Park, near Worcester.

Wye Valley Open Farm, Goodrich, near Ross-on-Wye. Open Easter-October.

BATHS AND SPORTS CENTRES.

Bromsgrove Swimming Pool, School Drive, off Stratford Road.

Hereford Leisure Centre, Holmer Road.

Hereford Swimming Baths Complex, St. Martin's Street.

Nunnery Wood Sports Centre, Spetchley Road, Worcester.

Perdiswell Sports Centre, Bilford Road, Worcester.

St. John's Sports Centre, Swanpool Walk, St. John's, Worcester.

Worcester Bath, Sansome Walk, Worcester.

OTHER INFORMATION ON WALKING IN HEREFORD AND WORCESTER.

For details of guided walks, contact:

Hereford & Worcester County Council, County Hall, Spetchley Road, Worcester, WR5 2NP (Tel: 0995 353366)

For a schedule of walk description sheets in the Malvern area, contact:

The Hon. Secretary, Mapping Section, Malvern Hills District Footpath Society, 5 Lansdowne House, Madresfield Road, Great Malvern, Worcs. WR14 2AS.

FOR BUS AND RAIL TIMETABLES, contact:

Castleways Coaches, Greet Road, Winchcombe, Glos. (0242-603715).

Midland Red West Ltd., Heron Lodge, London Road, Worcester. (0905-359353).

British Rail (Worcester 27211 8am-8pm - 021643 2711 (24 hours).

TOURIST INFORMATION CENTRES.

Bromsgrove, 49 Worcester Road. Tel: 0527 31809.

Bromyard, 1 Rowberry Street. Tel: 08852 82341.

City of Hereford, Shire Hall. Tel: 0432 68430.

City of Worcester, Guildhall, High Street. Tel: 0905 723471 (Ex. 202).

Droitwich Spa Heritage Centre, Heritage Way. Tel: 0905 774312.

Evesham Almonry Museum, Abbey Gate. Tel: 0386 6944.

Kington, Council Offices, 2 Mill Street. Tel: 0544 230202.

Ledbury, Council Offices, St. Katherine's, High Street. Tel: 0531 2461.

Leominster, School Lane. Tel: 0568 6460.

Leominster, 3 The Grange. Tel: 0568 2291.

Malvern Hills, The Winter Gardens, Great Malvern. Tel: 06845 2700.

Pershore, Council Offices. Tel: 0386 554711.

Ross-on-Wye, 20 Broad Street. Tel: 0989 62768.

Tenbury Wells, Teme Street. Tel: 0584 810136.

Scarthin Books of Cromford are the leading Peak District specialists in secondhand and antiquarian books, and purchase good books, music, maps and photographs at fair and informed valuations.
Contact Dr. D. J. Mitchell by letter, or phone Wirksworth 3272.

THE FAMILY WALKS SERIES

General Editor: Norman Taylor

Family Walks in the White Peak. Norman Taylor 1985. Reprinted 1985. Revised 1987. ISBN 0 907758 09 6.
Judged by 'The Great Outdoors' to be: "the best Peak District short walks guide yet published."

Family Walks in the Dark Peak. Norman Taylor 1986. Revised 1988. ISBN 0 907758 16 9.
Companion to the first title in the Series.

Family Walks in the Cotswolds. Gordon Ottewell 1986. Revised 1988. ISBN 0 907758 15 0.
Covers the area between Gloucester and Stow-on-the-Wold.

Family Walks around Bristol, Bath and the Mendips. Nigel Vile 1987. ISBN 0 907758 19 3.

Family Walks in the Downs and Vales of Wiltshire. Nigel Vile 1988. ISBN 0 907758 21 5.

Family Walks in South Yorkshire. Norman Taylor 1989. ISBN 0 907758 25 8.

Family Walks in the Wye Valley. Heather and John Hurley 1989. ISBN 0 907758 26 6.
From Haye-on-Wye to Chepstow.

Family Walks in Mid-Wales. Laurence Main 1989. ISBN 0 907758 27 4.
Between Snowdonia and the Brecon Beacons.

Ready Spring 1990

Family Walks in Shropshire. Marian Newton. ISBN 0 907758 30 4.

Family Walks in North Staffordshire. Les Lumsdon. ISBN 0 907758 34 7.

Family Walks in Cheshire. Chris Buckland. ISBN 0 907758 29 0.

Family Walks in South Gloucestershire. Gordon Ottewell. ISBN 0 907758 33 9.

Family Walks in South Devon and Dartmoor. John Bainbridge. ISBN 0 907758 31 2.

Family Walks in Snowdonia. Laurence Main. ISBN 0 907758 32 0.

The Publishers D. J. Mitchell and E. G. Power welcome suggestions for further titles in this series and will be pleased to hear from suitably experienced walkers.